BUILDING BETTER BOARDING KENNELS

AND OTHER SUCCESSFUL PET INDUSTRY BUSINESSES

LAURA VINOGRADOV

HoboTCK
—— MEDIA ——

Paperback: ISBN 979-8-9877917-8-3

TABLE OF CONTENTS

Chapter 1.
INTRODUCTION

So, you want to own your own pet care business? Of course you do. You love animals. You probably have had pets in your life, you love them to the moon and back, and you want to spend all your days taking care of other peoples' animals. What could be better than spending your days with puppies and kittens *while earning a living*?

But... if the only reason you have for starting a pet care business is because you love puppies and kittens (or other adorable pets) and nothing would please you more than to care for these little bundles of joy... or if your goal is to play all day with kittens and puppies (or other adorable pets) and make a little money while doing so... leave now. Don't walk away. RUN! Run for your very life because this is not how owning or managing a pet care business works. Not by a long shot.

Before you spend any more time on this fantasy, you need to hear the following with no sugar coating. Because none of that happens when you are a business owner in pet care.

Caring for your own pets is work. A lot of work. Professional pet care is harder. Running your own pet care business is harder still. Running a *successful* business in the pet industry is hardest of all. While caring for any animal is a huge responsibility, caring for other people's pets is a crushing responsibility.

Do you already have a pet but want to do more? Go volunteer with a rescue or shelter. They may let you play with the puppies all day, but realistically, even *they* will probably expect you to actually work, and that will mean doing the grunt work, aka: cleaning poop, washing food and water bowls, cleaning cages. But at least at the end of

1

your shift you can go home and relax. You will be able to take weekends off, go on vacation whenever you want, and when you are sick, you will be able to stay home without a care in the world. These things do not happen when it comes to running a business in the pet industry.

However, if you are interested in creating and running a *successful* and *sustainable* business *AND ARE WILLING TO DO THE WORK*, stick around! And keep reading.

The key to building and running a pet-related business is to acknowledge that it is first and foremost a business and needs to be treated as such.

There may be, and almost certainly will be, many holiday celebrations and family meals missed. You will lose sleep. You will worry about the mistakes you have made, the near disasters, and you will likely obsess over the "what ifs". Markets and economies change. Competition is a constant challenge. And animals are predictable only to a point.

While it may not require a college degree, working with animals and running a business that focuses on pets do require a vast body of knowledge. You will be challenged to use that knowledge every day. It may require you to learn a completely new skill set. It certainly requires a lot of hard work and a 24/7 commitment.

There are laws to follow, goals to meet, and expenses to be paid. Lights need to be kept on, licensing and permits need to be secured. Depending on your specific niche and specific business, animals need to be fed and vet bills are inevitable. Your staff will need to be paid. And unless you are independently wealthy, you will also need to pay yourself a salary.

It can all be a little scary.

Yet, despite all the challenges and struggles, it can be

done. I know because I've done it.

The information you will find in this book is based on years of research, trial and error, and decades of experience (mine and others').

Back in 2006, when I first had the idea to open a pet care business, I was where you are today. A lifetime of caring for dogs and decades of working with them for my own enjoyment led me to finally choose to work professionally in this industry. As I set off on this path, I knew (or thought I knew) precisely what I wanted my business to look like and how I wanted it run because I had seen the good, the bad, and the ugly of pet care over the years.

In truth, I originally planned to build a doggy daycare. But my research, and some very restrictive local ordinances, made me shift gears and I opened a dog boarding kennel instead. That research saved me immeasurable time and money. And it made me stop to think about what else I didn't know. Because despite the vast knowledge and many skills I brought to the table, there was so much I still needed to learn!

I had a major advantage when it came to doing market research as I had worked as a journalist for years and the cornerstone of all good journalism is research. My marketing skills, which saved me thousands of dollars, also came via my journalism work.

But even with all that, I could not have done this alone. I was fortunate to have family members to mentor me in areas where I lacked experience and others who stepped up throughout the process with their suggestions, points of view, and manual labor. And even with all this expertise and support, it was still a huge leap of faith, because the timing could not have been worse.

I bought the property for my boutique kennel just as the

Chapter 1.

Great Recession hit the US in 2008. The physical building of my kennel facility got underway the following March. On the one hand, the bad economy freed up the laborers and subcontractors I needed to help build the kennel facility. But I had many sleepless nights worrying that this would all blow up in my face.

The Barking Lot opened for business in May 2009 and all my research proved itself and the pet industry proved its resilience.

I mitigated my risk somewhat by starting out slowly with just nine runs and no employees other than one of my daughters. Six months later, by that November, we were scrambling to finish the last of the originally planned-for twenty runs as we were bursting at the seams and began welcoming our Thanksgiving guests.

Next, the kennel expanded to include a small retail shop and became the local hub for carefully curated pet supplies. I had also become a local guru for those wanting to feed their dogs a raw diet. The grooming room was completed and an experienced professional groomer was hired.

Within nine months of opening, the business was debt-free. By the beginning of year three, I felt confident in the sustainability of the business and I began to hire back-of-house kennel staff. In short order there was a payroll of up to seven full- and part-time employees, depending on the season.

The business was a success! I had done it. And you can do it, too!

As you progress through this book and as you start your business, try not to underestimate yourself. You are entering this field with your own body of knowledge, your already-acquired skill sets, and your own experience caring for animals. Use those as starting points and keep learning. This book is a great place to start that learning process and hopefully it will remain a resource for you for a long time.

The first few chapters of this book focus on starting and running a business, any business.

The balance of this book walks you through setting up and maintaining specific businesses in the pet industry, including: dog walking, pet sitting, grooming, training, pet transportation, professional pet photography, pet product manufacturing, pet supply retail, pet rescues, doggy daycares and of course, boarding kennels.

After completing the chapters on running any business, you might be tempted to jump to the chapter that focuses on the specific business you are planning to build and read little else. I suggest that you don't.

It really is worth reading all the chapters, even if you think they might never apply to you. Just because you are planning to be a professional groomer does not mean you should avoid learning about boarding kennels; you might find yourself working at a boarding kennel as their in-house groomer and it would be helpful to understand their point of view. Alternatively, as a groomer you might want to supplement your income with pet sitting during your grooming slow season. Investing the time to learn about a variety of related businesses and business models may open doors you never considered entering.

Each profession and each business has slightly different and specific needs. Understanding them will make you a better member of the wider pet industry community and will make you a better business owner in your niche.

Regardless of which sector of the pet industry you choose, there are challenges to running your own business:

Chapter 1.

- You will work harder than you ever have before
- It's very hard to take vacations, and you can kiss sick days goodbye
- You may have to fire people (it's not easy)
- You may be stuck with clients you don't like (at least for a while)
- You are responsible for every dollar in and every dollar spent
- All decisions fall on your shoulders

But let's not overlook the upsides:

- You reap the benefits of your own work
- You can set your own schedule
- You can eventually control your client list (you get to "fire" bad clients)
- Only _you_ set your limits for expanding revenues
- You make all the decisions
- You can never be fired
- Occasionally you get to play with cute puppies and kittens!

Before we get into the thick of things, you should be aware of the one key factor to succeeding in pet care that will make or break your business, regardless of your business savvy:

Trust.

Trust is everything in pet care. *Everything.*

Trust is hard to earn and almost impossible to regain once lost. Your reputation is worth its weight in gold and more. Many, if not most, of your prospective clients will check around before hiring you or buying your product or services. Only those who trust you will recommend you. Break their trust even once, and they may never return.

Never over-promise, always fulfill your promises, and never, ever put your business ahead of the safety and security of the animals in your care or for whom you are developing products or services. If you want to succeed and prosper in pet care, earn people's trust.

If after reading this introduction you still want to move forward and have your own pet-related business, congratulations! You are going to be great!

Welcome to the wonderful, crazy world of the pet industry!

Good luck!

Laura

Chapter 2.
ARE YOU SURE?

Hopefully, you have chosen to become a professional in the pet industry because you genuinely love animals. That is a great motivator, but it cannot be the only reason to start or run a business in pet care. Love of animals is simply not enough if you want to succeed. Never forget for a moment that this is a business, and in order for your business to be profitable, you have to attend to the business end of things or hire someone to do it. Entrepreneurship is not for everyone. Here's why:

Start-ups require an almost impossible amount of time and work. Running your own business, even after it has taken hold does, too. You will forever be juggling home life and work. There is a seemingly never-ending to-do list. Some of these tasks are fun, some you will love or learn to love. Others you will never enjoy but they still need doing. The challenge for every business owner is getting them all done.

Let's say you are a groomer. If you work as an employee for someone else, your to-do list is relatively short. You show up, get handed a list of pets to groom, pull out your equipment, and groom all day. Then, after sweeping up and cleaning your own tools, you go home. You may have to file taxes once a quarter if you are a subcontractor; if you are a full-on employee, you will not even have to do that. At the end of the week, you simply pick up your paycheck. You are responsible for your own personal tools, but everything else is handed to you. Someone else markets the business and brings in the clients. Someone else pays the bills. It can be physically hard but at the end of the day, after the last pet is picked up and the grooming room swept up, you go home.

Alternatively, let's take a look at what a typical day for your imaginary grooming shop might look like, when you are the business owner.

You will: pay bills; make (or check) yesterday's deposits; make sure you have petty cash and change for cash transactions (which might mean a dash to the bank). You will check your internet connection, your website, and check that your payment apps are working. You will order marketing materials; do inventory; and order supplies. At least once a month you will need to speak with your CPA (Certified Public Accountant) and get receipts to them. Then you will retrieve and respond to customers' emails, texts, and voice messages; go through all your other business-related emails; pay salaries. And all that is before you open the doors for the day. Before your first client shows up, long before you pick up your scissors to actually groom, you will have already put in a full day's work.

Once your business-focused to-do list is completed, you can open the doors, invite in your first client, and begin to groom, right? Maybe not quite yet.

You still have to empty the dryer of yesterday's towels, fold them and put them away; refill shampoo bottles; possibly refine the order you placed earlier that morning; check your equipment; reserve the services of your local blade sharpener; check, clean, and restock the bathroom; sweep or vacuum and then dust (unless you stayed late to do that yesterday); take out yesterday's trash; listen to your employees' issues; set out their schedule for the day; and then maybe you can begin to groom.

What about growing your business? That, too, needs to be attended to almost daily, usually at the end of a very long day.

Chapter 2.

You will: respond to inquiries; investigate new opportunities for marketing and advertising; organize the photos you took all day for social media; create content for social media and advertising; post to social media; network within the industry; network within your community; look for ways to expand your business or add revenue streams.

Would you like to see how that translates into a 24-hour day?

Task	Hours per day
Attend to current business:	2 (at least)
Attending to future business:	2 (at least)
Actually doing your job:	8-10
Eating:	3
Personal Hygiene:	2
Errands, House & Car:	1 (probably more)
Sleep:	8 (probably a lot less)
TOTAL	**26 -28 hours!**

That is no less than 26 hours of activity in a 24-hour day! Are you freaking out yet? Maybe just a little? Take a breath. Others have done it and so can you.

You *can* run your business while doing your job. It comes down to knowing what needs doing and getting organized. The ability to multitask helps. In fact, it is probably imperative.

One way to be sure you are attending to all aspects of your business, and leaving nothing to fall between the cracks, is by obsessive list-keeping. Start by creating a checklist with three categories: a) the Business End of Your Business; b) Building (and Then Growing) Your Business; and c) Doing Your Job.

Now, make a list of each and every action item related to each category, no matter how mundane, no matter how small, and no matter how long the list. The more detailed your list is, the better. Your to-do list will be based on the requirements for your specific business. For instance, boarding kennels start their day by letting dogs out to relieve themselves and cleaning runs, followed by feeding breakfast. A pet supply retail store has none of these action items but may have daily deliveries of inventory that need unloading and shelves that need restocking. A doggy daycare may need to mow the grass most mornings before their guests arrive.

Your to-do list will be long; it may be extremely long. The tasks may seem unending and overwhelming. But know this: *all* start-ups are overwhelming at first, even for experienced entrepreneurs. It takes time to get into the groove of any new business. Getting organized takes time. Soon, certain things will become second nature and won't take so long.

Knowing what needs your attention and what needs doing comes down to planning. Planning is key.

Planning a business starts long before finding a name, creating a logo, and certainly before buying custom T-shirts. It takes time, effort, and research to make realistic and viable plans.

Doing the homework that will give rise to your business plan may sound a bit boring, but it doesn't have to be. You may even be surprised how interesting the process is and how much you like it! But even if you never come to love the nuts and bolts behind the scenes, it is beyond necessary; it is the "everything". It is the foundation on which your business will stand. By putting in the time and doing your homework before you spend or risk any money, you will be far better prepared to avoid pitfalls and setbacks, and possible failure.

There are four steps any budding entrepreneur should take

before ordering those cute T-shirts you've already designed in your mind's eye and already imagined wearing proudly around town.

1. Do some self-examination. Ask and answer yourself honestly why you want to do this.
2. Be able to state clearly what your goals are and what success would look like for you.
3. Write a coherent plan.
4. Find a "travel buddy" if you possibly can for this very exciting, and possibly bumpy, ride.

STEP ONE: SELF-EXAMINATION

The very first question you should ask yourself before embarking on creating a business, any business, is: Why? Why do you want to open your own business? There are easier ways to earn an income. Why take on that responsibility and all that risk? To be able to weather the challenges of starting up and difficult times, you need to be sure of why you got into this in the first place.

1. For many people, owning their own business answers a need to be their own boss. Not all of us are built to take orders from others.
2. There are business owners who may not have had any intention of ever being entrepreneurs but, seeing needs not being met or opportunities being missed, decided that they want to fill those gaps.
3. Some people see running their own show as an opportunity to express their creativity, while other entrepreneurs want to take a proven concept and improve on it.
4. There are people who are in it solely for a large financial payoff; budding entrepreneurs who want to build a business, or an empire, to make more money than any salary can provide.

5. And sometimes, starting one's own business is born out of necessity when other employment opportunities do not exist.

There is no "right" reason to start one's own business. Just be sure you are honest with yourself as to why you are taking this leap. Because no matter what your reasons, understanding why you want to do this will allow you to clearly define your achievable goals.

Knowing what your goals are will direct many of your decisions; and you will have countless decisions that need to be made. Seeing how those decisions will help or hinder you from achieving your goals will go a long way toward helping you make the right choices. Focusing on your goals will also help get you through the tough times. We'll look into goal-setting a little later in this chapter.

Next, consider all your experience to gauge how steep your learning curve will be and how much help you will need. Be honest; dishonest or less-than-thoughtful answers will only hurt you. The questions you need to ask yourself depends somewhat on whether or not you have owned (not just run) your own business before. And if you did, did you build it from scratch or buy it ready-made?

Ask yourself:

1. What was it like running your own business? What did you enjoy about it? What did you hate?

2. What business skills do you bring to the table? How much will you need to contract out?

List every single skill and talent you can offer. Some may not seem entirely relevant, but it is really too early in the process to know that for sure. Is organization your "superpower"? Put that on your list. Are you detail oriented? Are you strong in analysis and modeling? Are you a good listener, have the ability to push through exhaustion, recover from setbacks quickly? All these skills and talents may come into play. Heck, even speaking additional languages might be an asset.

Spend some time thinking about your negative characteristics as well. Be honest. No one is good at all things. Knowing what your weaknesses are, gives you an opportunity to work on them or, when you can, to hire someone who can compensate for them.

Assess all your tangible and intangible skill sets as well as your character and temperament. Take a good look at what you bring to the table that might help you in this endeavor. Think about how exactly each skill or talent adds value. Assess those things you lack. Do you have time to learn the skills you lack for this new business? If not, how will you fill in the gaps?

STEP TWO: KNOW WHAT YOUR GOALS ARE
Before "hanging out your shingle" you should be able to answer, "What are my goals?" Your goals may change over time, but unless you know what success looks like, how will you know if you've succeeded or not? Be specific. Avoid vague, generic so-called goals.

EXAMPLES OF GENERIC, NON-SPECIFIC GOALS:
- "If I could work with horses all day, I'd be so much happier"

- "I am passionate about animals and want to work with them"

- "I want to get rich"

Instead, articulate tangible goals that are specific and measurable.

EXAMPLES OF SPECIFIC GOALS:
- I want to work full time as an animal trainer in the entertainment industry.

- I want to keep my present job but supplement my income by pet sitting on the weekends.

- I make the best homemade pet food and I want to get it on every pet store shelf so others can benefit from it.

- I want to build a boarding kennel, run it with my family, and leave it to my children.

Notice that these goals do not address how much profit you want to make or how large you want your business to be. All that will come later. Promise.

STEP THREE: GET A TRAVEL PARTNER FOR THE JOURNEY
If you or your business would do better with a second set of hands or a skill set you neither have or are interested in acquiring, or if you simply want to share this experience with someone, get a partner. Just be careful about whom you choose.

Different work styles can be complementary but can also be a constant source of conflict that can hurt a business. Your good friend may not remain your friend for long if you are always arguing about money or work decisions. Honest discussions, even heated ones, are great and necessary. Arguing because each of you have completely different world views is often detrimental. Meanwhile, a complete stranger can become a friend through growing a business together.

In choosing a partner, focus on how you two complement each other and bring different skills to the table. Have similar goals. Be clear about who does what and how conflicts will be resolved (because conflicts and disagreements will certainly arise).

Chapter 2.

No matter who your partner is, if there is an imbalance of investments, be clear how that impacts profits and the decision-making process. In short, communicate!

Even if you do not need a co-pilot, you should do your best to have a support system in place before you begin. This can be friends, family, or others in the same boat as you (yes, even competitors can support one another). If your plan is to fly solo, find someone to mentor you. If you can't find a mentor, find a colleague in a related field and support one another. Use each other as sounding boards for ideas and for venting when things get rough.

Starting a new business is hard; starting a new business completely alone is a very, very heavy burden to carry by yourself.

STEP FOUR: WRITE IT DOWN
Writing a business plan is not rocket science but it is methodical work. It can sound intimidating and it may be difficult for you at first. Don't get discouraged; others have done it and you can, too. The next two chapters will walk you through the process of developing and writing a business plan.

By writing an actual document describing what you learned and how it applies to the business you have envisioned, you will have a document to refer to, measure your journey by, and that will hold you accountable, even if that's just to yourself. It will include your goals and targets and it will include a budget. Actually writing down your business plan, as opposed to "keeping it all in your head," will make the theoretical real. It will confirm or deny the viability of your ideas.

Do not make the mistake that planning your business is "one and done". Your business plan is your road map and your touchstone. Like all good road maps, it merely points you in the right direction. When circumstances change, so must your map.

The best advice ever given regarding business planning is this:

> *"If you want to succeed you need to know three things. The first is where you are. The second is where you want to go. And the third is how you are going to get there."*

This is the essence of a business plan: To know where you are, knowing where you want to go, and figuring out how to get there.

Write it down.

Refer back to your business plan regularly.

Chapter 3.
MARKET RESEARCH FOR ANY BUSINESS

Underpinning all successful businesses is market research. Without market research you will be flying blind, which may work for a while, but rarely ends well in the long term. Without properly researching every aspect of your new business and the market, you could invest hard-earned savings and a lot of time and effort, only to find that your business is not sustainable or may never get off the ground at all. This could be due to a badly chosen location, prices your target market will not pay, unforeseen expenses, or out-right rejection of your products or services because they have not been manufactured properly or that they are simply items that no one wants.

The fact is that a majority of businesses fail. And many of those businesses that have failed, offered great services or products.

Your great product or service needs to find its paying customers. You need to identify your target market and identify what motivates them. You need to know how to reach them. You need to be sure that those specific customers will pay the prices you intend to charge and that those prices are enough to cover your expenses and provide a profit.

You need to do market research.

Good market research will give you all the vital information you need to begin. Great market research should show you your path forward today and for some time to come.

RESEARCH
Every serious business plan is based on data. Collect as

much data and information as you can. Be sure to do good research, quality counts. Do not rely on the first set of statistics and data you come across. Check and verify every bit of information you intend to rely on. As you research and collect information, consider the source of all that data. Even internal industry statistics may or may not be accurate.

You might encounter "inflation" and "position creep". Industries and businesses like to present themselves in the rosiest terms possible. There is a difference between reporting accurate figures to tax authorities and exaggerating a bit for public consumption. It's the public consumption number that gets picked up and reported, and re-reported, until it eventually takes on the aura of fact. Just because it's written somewhere does not make it a fact, no matter how many times you encounter the same narrative. You will almost certainly find many sources presenting identical information and statistics. Seeing the same data over and over again *may* signal their veracity and accuracy; or it could mean that all these sites are relying on a single source with possibly faulty or inflated data. Be wary of data that is repeated blindly.

While you work your way through mountains of information, work methodically. Create a file system that works for you and protect it.

- Organize the material you find useful and save it.

- Take lots of notes and save them.

- Be sure to save the bibliographical information (where did you find the information, when, who wrote it, who published it). You will need this if you reference that material later on. And if you are ever challenged (or simply want to review your information) you will know where to find it.

Chapter 3.

Even with the ease and convenience of the internet, this research could take weeks. It could take longer. While it is tempting to rush the process, do not cut corners. Even if you choose to use AI platforms to do your searches for you, you still need to read and absorb the information. Take the time to go down as many rabbit holes as possible.

The goal of all this research is to become an expert about your business and the industry or sector in which it exists. Will there always be more to learn? Of course. But once you can discuss your business and its environment coherently and confidently, you can begin to synthesize it into a narrative (your business plan).

Market research is never done, but at some point you need to take what you have and go for it. How will you know you have reached that point?

You will know you are ready to start writing when you:

- You have a solid understanding, from a bird's eye view, of your industry and the niche you are interested in, within that industry.

- Have defined your target market.

- Understand how your industry functions in your area and within your target market.

- Know your business' realistic potential.

- Know, from A-to-Z, precisely what your product (or service) is and how does it meet a need.

- Know the price points for your product or service.

- Know who your competitors are and uncover what makes them successful (or not).

- Can articulate the challenges you face today; what might the challenges of the future look like; and how will you deal with them.

Where to begin?

OVERVIEW OF YOUR INDUSTRY

Start your research with an overview of the pet industry. While you do not need to be an expert about every single aspect of all pet-related businesses, it will benefit you to know as much as you can about the industry in general and to know about other related sectors.

After you learn about the very broad pet-industry (and it is broad and diverse), spend even more time learning about the sector you are focusing on. You want to have a thorough understanding of:

- The history of your market niche within the industry. You can learn a lot from knowing where it has been.

- The current market, its size and scope, and its projected future.

- The region you plan to work in: its size and scope, its population, and demographics.

- Where are the opportunities and barriers. Learn what others have tried but that did not work; uncover what clients are looking for or complaining about.

- Competitors and their strengths and weaknesses. Underestimating your competition usually results in bad decisions being made and bad outcomes. If you cannot find a direct competitor, look into those outside your immediate area but who work in your intended niche.

Chapter 3.

- Where can you and your business fit in.

MARKET SHARE

Once you have a firm grasp on the size of the overall market and the size of the market niche where your business will reside, you should research your business' potential market share. It takes a lot of bravado and a sizeable ego to declare that your business will outperform your established competition by all matrices and you will soon control 20, 30, 50 percent of the market. Statements like these usually point to a lack of knowledge.

At the same time, it also points to an uninformed naiveté to say, "I'll be happy with 2% of the market share", thinking that it is such a small amount that surely it is an achievable goal. In reality, depending on your business, a two percent market share can be a lot and may take years to achieve. Two percent of the U.S. population is approximately 6.6 million people and that's a lot of customers! Two percent of the entire U.S. pet industry is $2.74 billion! Alternatively, two percent could be so small that, while achievable, your business would not survive at that level.

To know what a reasonable target market share is, you need to know what the market shares are for your competition, how long it took to get them there, and what impacted them achieving or losing market share. Only then will you be able to plan accordingly.

RESEARCH YOUR BUSINESS (SERVICE OR PRODUCT) ITSELF

This may sound counterintuitive but you need to research your own business, thoroughly. In order to plan properly, you need to know, really know, every aspect of your future business inside and out.

Learn everything you can about:

- Each and every product you plan to sell. Know where and how it is manufactured. Learn every component and ingredient. Familiarize yourself with every step in the process of production, shipping, storing, and transportation of the product. And be very sure about any and all regulations regarding any product you sell or intend to manufacture.

- Each and every service you plan to offer. Know what education or skills are needed to provide that service. Learn what constitutes good service and what are the challenges in providing that high quality of service.

- Every component and every step it will take to start and run your business. Learn how long it might take to build your facility or receive licensing. What will rent or a mortgage cost? What will transportation costs be? How many employees will you need and how much each employee will cost and is worth (how much revenue they generate)? Know what equipment and supplies you will need and what they will cost.

- Who your potential vendors are and what support services will be necessary.

- All the regulations that may come into play while setting up or while running your business. Any number of governmental agencies may have jurisdiction over your business. Know precisely which ones do. Learn what it takes to be and stay in compliance. Mistakes can be costly.

It is very important that your research reflects your specific business *in your specific location*. Knowing what the data is for a similar business half-way around the world is possibly, if not likely, worthless.

<u>LEARN ABOUT SALES AND MARKETING</u>
Spend time learning about Sales and Marketing. While they go hand in hand, they are not the same. Marketing is how you reach your audience; sales closes deals.

You do not need a degree in marketing to have a successful business but you should understand the goals and motivations behind marketing as well as how to create and execute marketing campaigns. Even if you intend to hire someone to oversee the business' marketing plan that you create, you should be knowledgeable about what that job requires and how to measure success.

The same goes for sales and sales campaigns. Even if you intend to hire someone to oversee your sales department, you should be knowledgeable about what that job requires and how to measure success.

Marketing and sales planning must be data driven and collecting data requires a lot of research. If you cannot afford original market research, find research done by others. Whether the data is collected by you or others, you need to internalize the following:

- What motivates people to act. This might mean doing a short deep-dive into psychology and sociology research.

- What motivates people, particularly those in your target market, to buy.

- What are your marketing avenues and how might each one benefit your business. From social media to traditional media advertising, there are numerous possibilities for reaching your target customers. Learn which are most effective for you by learning about them all.

- What are the costs associated with the various marketing and sales options available for your target audience.

- Learn what sales strategies are best suited for your business and what each strategy offers.

LEARN HOW TO CREATE BUDGETS

Would you believe it if you were told that entire business plans could be reduced to their budgets? Well, to some degree they can. Entrepreneurs and investors well-versed in reading budgets can all but skip the narrative portion of business plans and understand where that business is, where it is going, and how it is going to get there, just by reading the numbers. A well-developed budget is just that powerful.

If you have never created one before, take some time to learn the ABCs of budgets. Learn what is included and what is not. Familiarize yourself with what they look like and learn to read them. This can be intimidating at first and even confusing. Try to find someone who is "fluent" in budgets who is willing to walk you through a few. It shouldn't matter which industries they come from. Once you can read and understand one budget, you can understand them all.

There are many different budget models and you need to find the one that works best for you. You could invest in highly sophisticated software, but a basic Excel spreadsheet works great, too.

You will want to build a budget that will work for now, for a year from now, and for five years from now. Gather enough information to do that. While you cannot predict the future, you can amass enough data to make educated guesses. Then enter that data into your budget and see where it takes you.

Chapter 3.

BUDGET ITEMS FOR A PET INDUSTRY BUSINESS

What goes into a business budget? Basically, you want to include every business expense and every source of income.

Expenses generally include:

- CODB (Cost Of Doing Business). These are the fixed items you are obliged to pay: rent or mortgages, utilities, internet, local taxes, licenses, mandatory memberships, equipment, taxes, vendors, loans, supplies, payroll

- Flexible expenses (i.e.: industry organizations' memberships, marketing budget items such as travel). These are items you have the most flexibility to increase or decrease

- Less flexible, but not fixed expenses such as repairs and upgrades

- Depreciation (equipment and facilities)

Your budget should also include sheets with your various sources of revenue.

Revenues include:

- The income from the sale of all the core goods and products you sell

- The income from any and all of the core services you provide

- Any and all income from secondary, additional revenue streams

LET'S GET SPECIFIC

What are the specific items you will need to account for in your budget? Here are many, but not necessarily all, of what needs to be included in yours.

- General Administration
  - Office
  - Rent or Mortgage
  - Office Supplies and Equipment
  - Cleaning supplies
  - Utilities (electric, gas, water, sewer costs)
  - Phone/Internet (communications installation, set up, and maintenance)
  - Insurance
  - Liability
  - Real Estate & Equipment
- Licensing and permits
  - Operational permits
  - Business Licenses
- Professional Services
  - Legal
  - Accounting
  - CPA
  - Payroll Company
  - Architect
  - Contractors
  - Compliance
  - Trade organization memberships
- Web & Software
  - Cloud hosting fees
  - Software licenses / usage fees
  - Backup and storage fees
  - 3rd party customer support fees

- o Mobile apps
- Sales and Marketing Costs
  - o Travel
  - o Entertainment
  - o Employee Bonuses
  - o Discounts
- Sales (Labor)
  - o Sales Manager
  - o Sales staff
- Marketing
  - o Collateral development and production (content, videos, print)
  - o Website creation and maintenance
  - o Trade expos participation
  - o Events
  - o Advertising
  - o Old Media (TV, radio, print)
  - o New Media (social media)
  - o Loyalty Program
  - o Franchising
- Marketing (Labor)
  - o Marketing Manager
  - o Market Researcher
  - o PR/SEO/MarCom
  - o Customer support
  - o Loyalty program Manager
  - o Franchises sales support
  - o Customer service

- On site Labor Costs
  - Front of House
  - Facility Manager
  - Supervisor
  - Retail Manager
  - Back of House
  - Lead Pet Attendant
  - Pet Attendants
  - Groomers
  - Trainers
  - Instructors
  - Drivers
  - IT support
  - Assistants
  - Logistics staff
  - Cleaning crew
  - Maintenance
  - Landscaping
- Products
  - Product development
  - Production/Manufacturing (products, packaging)
  - Logistics (Warehousing, Shipping)
  - Compliance
- Management
  - CEO
  - CFO
  - Secretary

- o Bookkeeper
- o Comptroller

Some of these may not apply to your specific business and at the same time there may be other expenses not listed here.

Opposite and off-setting all those expenses are your revenues; that is, all your sources of income. These will include any number of the items below, depending on your actual business:

Revenues (Income)

- Boarding
  - o Overnight stays
  - o Add-ons (Pickup/delivery, meds dispensing, etc.)
- Doggy Daycare
  - o Day rate
  - o Add-ons (Pick up/delivery, special services)
- Dog Walking
  - o Proscribed fees
  - o Add-on services
  - o Sales of related equipment
- In-Home Pet Care
  - o Per day rate
  - o Add-ons
- Retail
  - o Brick-and-mortar or e-commerce sales
  - o Affiliate sales
- o Branded or Developed Products
  - o Sale of products

- o Wholesale sales
- o Licensing of products
- Relocation Services/Transportation
  - o Basic fees (per mile, per trip)
  - o Sale of travel equipment and materials
- Pet Training
  - o Registration fees for classes
  - o Facility sublease to a 3rd party instructor or group
  - o Sale of training equipment and supplies
- Photography Services
  - o Photography session bookings
  - o Sale of prints, holiday cards
  - o Royalties

It is unlikely that *all* of the revenue sources listed above will apply to you and your business. No one can do it all. So while some of these may not apply to your specific business, keep in mind that there may be multiple revenue streams to your business and you should account, or plan, for them all.

Once your budget is formatted with all the appropriate line items *for your specific business*, and populated with all the numbers your research has provided, you will know if your business is viable. It is better to do this before investing even more time and before you invest any money!

- If, based on your research and reasonable projections, your business would continually operate at a loss, you will need to reevaluate and rework your plan.

Do not let an initial loss dissuade you from pursuing your dream. Many businesses operate at a loss initially. Be sure your budget extends far enough into the future so you can see where you will be after you give your business a fighting chance.

- If, given time, your future business operates in the black (at a profit) and provides you with the income and future profits you want, you will know this can work.

As tempting as it may be, do not use your budget to paint a rosy picture. As you build your budget, err on the side of overestimating expenses while in the income columns, be conservative in estimating future business' income. Or build your budget three times, each one based on a different scenario.

The first scenario will reflect worst-case outcomes: very few sales and skyrocketing expenses. This will allow you to see how long your business can survive under these terms. Scenario two is the best-case results. Your expenses remain precisely what the research says they are today, and sales are through the roof. The third scenario is the middle-ground where your expenses are somewhat accurate, and sales are decent.

FINAL THOUGHTS ABOUT BUDGETS

It isn't enough to compile and calculate numbers. It isn't enough to create a spreadsheet once and then ignore it. Understand and know your budget thoroughly!

You should:

- Learn your numbers.
- Trust your numbers.
- Check and review your budget repeatedly and often. Make adjustments to your budget to suit the reality you are faced with as often as necessary.

OTHER THINGS TO RESEARCH BEFORE YOU BEGIN TO WRITE YOUR BUSINESS PLAN

Your research should not hyperfocus on just finding data and information about what could be a rather narrow view of your business. Take time to think about and research a bigger picture.

- Additional revenue streams. There may be ways to add revenues without distracting from your core business. In fact, some of these options may add real value to your core business and not just provide an additional revenue stream. Adding a small retail corner to your boarding facility may convert a retail buyer into a boarding client, or vice versa. The same is true for adding training services. Come for the training, stay for the boarding.

- Investment options, opportunities, and costs. If you think your business can be best served by attracting outside investment, you should take the time to understand how investments actually work. Know the difference between VC (venture capital) and PE (private equity). Learn what options and warrants are and how they differ. Understand how much a bank loan will actually cost you.

- Your end game. Are you building this business to eventually sell it at a profit? You need to know at what point that might be realistic and what that will take. Do you intend to grow your small startup into a business that will trade on a stock exchange and then cash out? Even if you envision maintaining your business "forever", there will come a time for you to step back. What happens to your company then? You need to plan and in order to plan that, you need to research your viable options.

- Take lots of "field trips". Gathering information about your competition could be done from home, *or* you could go into their establishments and see for yourself what works for them and what appears to not work in their favor.
- Speak with people in the field regarding all aspects of your future business. They have the real world experience you lack and the internet might lack, too.

REMEMBER THAT:

- Knowledge is key. Know your industry, know your business from A to Z, backwards and forwards. Do your homework before you jump in.

- Take your time. Short cuts may come back to plague you.

- Learn from the successes and mistakes of others.

- Market research is never ending. Stay up-to-date with your industry and market trends. Attend professional events and conferences. Subscribe to industry publications. Follow industry experts on social media and engage with them and your fellow professionals.

Once your research is completed, then what? You sit down to actually write a business plan. But, before we move on to how to write a business plan, stop and consider what the research has shown.

Has the information you have uncovered support, or speak against, the business you *thought* you wanted? Is the business you envisioned still the one you want to launch? Have you changed your mind about anything regarding the business you set out to research? Are those changes small tweaks to the initial core concept or have you realized that what you thought you wanted to do completely morphed

into something else? Now is the time to put on the brakes
if you are no longer convinced that your initial concept
will work or if it is right for you. Be honest with yourself.
If the data points to weaknesses in your initial assessment,
do not be afraid to rethink, or even scratch, the entire
project.

Now is the time to either recalculate, pivot, or walk away.
Do not proceed with such a commitment if the data shows
it is not likely to succeed or if you no longer feel this is the
path for you. It is better you do this early, before you
invest any more time or money in something you are not
sure of.

But if your research bears out what your gut and heart
initially whispered, and you are just as passionate as
before, it's time to create your road map to get you where
you have been wanting to go. Let's write a business plan.

Chapter 4.
WRITING A BUSINESS PLAN

Lack of planning and a clear narrative can, and often does, lead to being underfunded, over-extended, or completely misunderstanding the market. It can lead to failure even for the best ideas and the best of intentions.

At a minimum, a business plan should not only explain how and why, it should address challenges seen and challenges anticipated. It should point out strengths and weaknesses in the market and in you. A good business plan sets down benchmarks and goals and gives the business owner and interested parties a road map and a framework by which to measure success.

Virtually no one could possibly hold all the previously researched information in their head. And even if you could, it would take hours and days to explain it all to a third party (potential partner, investor, banker). The point of the business plan is to take all the information and data amassed from the market research and put it into a document that organizes the data, provides an analysis of that information, and then constructs a clear narrative for starting, managing, and growing that business.

While there are generally accepted formats for arranging business plans, they are not "one size fits all". Obviously, different businesses, business sectors, and industries face different issues and challenges. The content of individual business plans must address the unique aspects of the business, the sector, and the industry in question.

Without a doubt, the pet industry and pet care is a unique market. It is somewhat like caring for children, but different. It requires a vast body of knowledge but appears to require low-skill labor. From the outside it looks like fun and games but decisions made can be life-altering for pets and their owners. There are special licensing and regulations specific for working with and on behalf of animals. Personal recommendations are its lifeline, more than most other industries. The list goes on and on. A business plan for a pet industry business needs to reflect all that, in addition to the basics that would be included for any business, regardless of industry.

Allowing for their diverse uses, business plans come in all shapes and sizes. They can run from a few pages long to a document of several hundred pages. The type and complexity of any business plan depends on what sort of business you are building as well as for whom you are writing the plan.

A plan for a solo dog-walking business written for the business owner's eyes only, will be short. The data still needs to be collected and analyzed; the game plan should still be as detailed as possible. But the narrative can be short and does not need to be eloquently written. This plan is a one-person road map.

However, if you are preparing to speak with bankers or investors to get money to build a large manufacturing facility, they will want to know that you understand your market and your business, where the money (their money) is going, and how you are going to repay it. They want numbers, but they also want to know you have a clear vision and understanding about your capabilities, and both your short-term and long-term plans. This business plan is both your roadmap and their checklist.

Despite any differences, all good business plans are alike in that they tell you where you are, where you are going, and how you are going to get there. They should include a narrative and a budget which mirrors the narrative. They should also include the story of who you are and who is traveling with you.

Step one of a business plan is to write a mission statement.

MISSION STATEMENTS

A mission statement condenses your business, and your vision for it, down to its most basic core. Most mission statements are between one and three sentences, never exceeding 100 words. The best mission statements are typically a single sentence.

Consider, for example, "Nancy's Grooming Shoppe is dedicated to keeping pets healthy and looking beautiful all year long," or "Good Kitty Food aims to be the gold standard in fresh, raw cat food." These are short and at a glance tell the reader who you are and the *raison d'etre* of your business. A mission statement is not a tagline. "Things go better with Coca Cola™" is a tagline. It targets consumers' emotions so they will buy. Taglines help make your brand stand out. Mission statements explain your business.

A good rule of thumb is: if you cannot articulate an accurate, succinct mission statement, you may not have a good grasp of what your company's core business is. Imagine you are at a pitch meeting with the most important person who could make or break your business. You are given 10 seconds to explain it. Go! It's not easy. Keep working your mission statement until it is no longer than a 10-second pitch that succinctly and accurately describes your business. Mission statements, while short, can take a long time to perfect.

Once you are happy with your mission statement or are very close to being happy with it (keep at it), you should begin thinking about the executive summary of the plan.

EXECUTIVE SUMMARY

Think of the executive summary as the introduction to, and overview of, your new endeavor.

The executive summary is longer than a mission statement of course, but it need not be excessively long; that will depend on your specific business and for whom you are writing your business plan. It might only take a few paragraphs; it might require many pages. But when completed, your executive summary should explain:

- what and where the market is
- what it is lacking
- what your services or products are and how your services or products fill a need that is lacking

Be sure to include details about market trends, its potential growth, and its current and future challenges.

Much of the information included in the executive summary will be repeated throughout the business plan. That's okay. The summary introduces the information; repeated use of that information in the plan reinforces it or applies it.

Depending on the intended audience, the executive summary can be more, or less, formal in its tone. If you are writing just for you, you can keep it casual. If this business plan is going to a third party, write more formally and clearly. No mistakes, no typos. Write at a professional level or hire someone to do that for you. Imagine a room full of people in suits sitting around a table discussing your executive summary and considering whether or not to invest or to approve a loan. If the executive summary does not catch their interest, is unprofessionally written, or is off-putting, it is unlikely that a banker or investor will proceed with the application.

Be honest and forthcoming in your executive summary. Leave out any data you have not verified, but do not leave out data that points to weaknesses; these you can address. Do not exaggerate.

<u>THE BODY OF THE BUSINESS PLAN</u>
Try to keep your narrative short so people will actually read it but make it as long as necessary. Cite sources. Attribute quotes and data.

Introduce your business. What is it and what do you plan to do? Explain where it is located, what your territory and reach are, how your business will be structured; and of course, how it will be funded. This could run you several pages; at the very least this section should be several paragraphs long and should be detailed. This section should mimic and expand on the Executive Summary.

Explain what your business sector is. If you are writing this plan for your eyes only, this may seem obvious. Write it down anyway. This may feel repetitive and it is. But if this plan might *ever* be shown to others, you definitely need that repetition. Go into some detail about the industry particularly if the reader will be someone from outside the industry. What is the industry; what is the size and scope; how is it growing; and where is it going, are questions that should be addressed. Cite your data.

Next, discuss how your business fits into the overall ecosystem. What needs are you filling? Where are the opportunities that others are missing? Discuss the opportunities and trends.

Opportunities include identifying areas where the current market is underserved, providing an opportunity for a new business (yours); key processes that may be lacking which you possess or can create; or intellectual property (or other resources) that the market has not had access to previously but that you possess. Emphasize openings in the market that no one else has seen or have been able to fill.

Introduce your competitors. There is no need to deride them, rather, this is where you acknowledge their presence and address what they may be lacking and that you and your new business will provide.

Discuss your and your business' weaknesses; include the challenges facing you. Do not be afraid to recognize those challenges. No situation is perfect and anyone considering investing in your business will want to know that you recognize this. Challenges or stress points could include things such as barriers to market entry (for example, capital requirements, technical barriers, patents, and process barriers) that the company needs to overcome. Other challenges might include risks inherent to your business that need to be mitigated such as lack of experienced staff or location. Address these honestly while explaining how you will remedy, or at least mitigate, them.

Painting an unrealistic, overly rosy picture of what lies ahead or ignoring the challenges facing you, does no one any good. Investors will think that you either did not do your homework or that you have something to hide. Bankers will think the same.

Now that the entire environment has been fleshed out, double back and review why your business is prepared to succeed.

This is a good point in the narrative to discuss branding. You may not have created a logo yet, but you can discuss your vision for positioning your company. This heralds back to your mission statement.

BRANDING

Your business plan should discuss your brand. Branding is creating a business that is instantly recognizable.

Chapter 4.

Discuss how you plan to brand your business in terms of your mission; explain how each step of the way you intend to live up to the ideal of your mission.

If you have a logo, include any documents regarding your ownership or registration of that logo. Include proof of protection for your business name and tagline. These should be trademarked or copyrighted (check with legal counsel).

After addressing who and what your business is, set down details about what you hope to achieve, that is, your objectives and goals and how you plan to achieve them.

OBJECTIVES, GOALS, ACTION ITEMS, AND THE STRATEGIES NEEDED TO ACHIEVE THEM

Your business plan should include specific and measurable goals. It will be against those goals that you will measure the trajectory of your business. Meeting goals is a measure of success; not meeting goals means reevaluating how you are running your business.

Typically, goals are set in terms of quarterly revenues, but they could also be based on how many new clients have entered into your client base or acquisition of market share. After presenting what those goals are, discuss why you think these goals are reasonable and achievable. Make sure your numbers, even projections, are based in reality. Check your budget.

Next, write a sales and marketing plan. This lets the reader see the practical steps you plan to take to reach your goals. Even if you are using your business plan as a roadmap that only you will see, having a list of ideas for marketing your business alongside a number of detailed campaigns for the first six months or a year, is a great way to keep yourself on track. If other people, such as investors, will be reading this document, you should flesh out all these steps and campaigns and explain each one in detail. Explain why your business will spend money for advertising in your local paper and not the regional one; or why your sales force needs to be on the road intensively only three months a year.

Go into some detail about actual marketing campaigns. This includes where you will promote your business, what collateral your will produce, what events you'll participate in, when you will run special deals, and what advertising campaigns you plan to pay for. Discuss even those marketing campaigns that have no expenses associate with them. You are painting a picture of where your company is allocating time and effort, not just funds. Explain your intentions to use:

- Social media: Discuss creating cross-posted targets, website creation and maintenance, and how you will maintain an online presence. If you have experience and talent in this area, include that in this narrative. If this will require staff to maintain, say that here but leave the cost of that employee to the budget to explain.

- Promotions and your sales force: Depending on the type of business you build, your sales force may be in-store clerks, or road warriors hustling sales. It could also be your reception desk attendants. Whatever it is, discuss their training and preparation, as well as what promotional materials you plan to incorporate.

- Events: Your research should have led you to suitable options for promoting your business at events. List them here. Briefly discuss why each one is worthy of consideration. The costs for these will be addressed in your budget.

Chapter 4.

- Networking: If you plan to join local networking groups (or do so online) or intend to make yourself available to civic or community groups, let the reader know this. Include a targeted schedule for this activity (once a week, a month, a quarter).

By setting down in writing a game plan for sales and marketing, you will have a checklist to use to compare action items completed, or not, against financial goals met or missed.

Finally, if you own a patent that is pertinent to your business, or have submitted an application for a patent, include those details in this narrative portion of your business plan.

YOUR BUDGET
This may be the most proprietary item in your business plan. Be selective who you share this with.

One common and acceptable way to share your financials without sharing your entire budget is to only provide the P&L (Profit and Loss) section of your budget in your business plan.

Alternatively, you can insert a section into your business plan that simply says, "Financials provided" to show the reader that you do indeed have the numbers; they simply are not yet privy to see them.

PERSONAL BIOS
Wrap up the entire narrative by including a short but relevant bio for everyone involved, including founding partners, key staff, mentors, and members of the board of directors. For each, write a short synopsis of their relevant education, business experience, experience in this field, and what they bring to the table.

That is all there is to writing a business plan.

Finished writing? Great! Now what?

Review your plan. Ask a few trusted friends to read it and give you feedback. If after reading it, your reviewers can clearly see where you are, where you want to go, and how you are going to get there, you will know that you now have a framework for creating your business.

A FEW NOTES ABOUT WRITING BUSINESS PLANS

- Good business plans show the way. Great business plans include the bumps in the road. Include the challenges and how you will deal with them.

- Do not overshare your business plan. It is intellectual property that could be of great interest to your competitors.

- Be professional about your competition. They do not need to be your enemies; they could be (or become) your friends and allies.

- Review and revise your business plan regularly.

Chapter 5.
ESTABLISHING A BUSINESS

Establishing a business in the pet industry is, for the most part, no different from setting up any other business, with a few industry-specific differences and details.

All businesses have both legal and functional components. All businesses need a space to work, a way to collect fees and pay bills, and tools to run the day to day activities of the business. All businesses require bank accounts, permits and licenses. But, because you will be working with or on behalf of animals, you will also need to be in compliance with other additional laws and guidelines.

ESTABLISHING A BUSINESS ENTITY
Regardless of the size or scope of the company you intend to build, you should create a business entity. This will provide you and your personal assets protection from a number of threats, including lawsuits. Choosing which type of business entity depends on a multitude of factors.

Among the most basic and well-known business entities are LLCs (Limited Liability Corporations) or S-Corps (Subchapter Corporations) but there are others. If you are unfamiliar with these terms, now is the time to learn about them. Search online for general information to understand what your options are. If, after all your best efforts, you are still not sure which is right for you and your specific circumstances, speak with the kind folks at the IRS (Internal Revenue Service). The IRS has representatives whose job is to help people like yourself. They will not make the final decision for you, but they can provide a lot of guidance. Their services are free.

Alternatively, if you can afford to, speak with a CPA or tax attorney before deciding which corporate structure is right for you. While you will likely be charged a fee to consult with one of these experts, it may be worth the money to fully understand your options. Try to get it right from the start. But know this: If at a later date you decide that your chosen structure is not working for you or your circumstances change, your business' type of legal structure can be changed. It might be a slight hassle, but it can be done.

The process of actually registering a small business can often be done by you without paying a third party to set it up. Contact your local, state, and regional governments, and check with which of their offices you need to register. There will be representatives in each of these offices who can direct you to which forms need to be filled out and which documents they need from you. These agencies are more than happy to help you with the formalities of setting up the business entity; it's what they are there for.

INSURANCE

Insurance is one of those things people hate to pay for but are relieved they have it when they need it. There are many different types of insurance, and each jurisdiction requires some. The amount of coverage you need should be thoroughly explained to you by your insurance provider through their agent.

Find an insurance agent you can trust and speak with them openly and honestly about all aspects of your business and be sure they completely understand its scope. Make sure this agent has experience working with businesses in this field; the risks and liability in pet care are unique. That's one of the reasons that it can be particularly challenging to find insurance coverage for some businesses in this sector because the risks are many.

If a pet owner's expectations aren't met, you can be sued. If a dog or other pet gets lost while in your care, you can be sued. If an employee gets hurt while working for you, you can be sued. If a pet food you've manufactured makes a pet sick... you can be sued. While you may not lose any of those suits, there is always a chance that you might. And the time and effort to litigate can be a far bigger drain than any insurance premium.

Do not forget to protect yourself as well as your business. If you get hurt while on the job, you will want to be covered with supplemental insurance as standard worker's compensation does not always cover the business' owner.

Of course, it is wise to shop around for the most comprehensive coverage for the best price, but keep in mind that when it comes to insurance, cheaper may not be better.

LICENSING AND PERMITS

No matter what your business is, you will in all likelihood need a business license and possibly more than that to be in legal compliance. Contact your local licensing offices. If you are not sure which offices to contact, ask the people who helped you register your business entity, they should know.

The staff at the licensing office will know precisely which licenses you need, and which agencies need to approve and oversee businesses dealing with animals. If you are told that no special licensing is required, get that in writing so that you don't find yourself out of compliance down the road, facing fines, or closure of your business.

Contrary to popular opinion, these agencies are not your enemy. They actually do want to encourage small businesses and they do want you to go on to become a successful, tax-paying member of the business community.

The individuals working in these offices may appear curt or unhelpful; if so, ask to speak with someone else. Or make a face-to-face appointment. Personal contact often works when a faceless phone call does not.

If your business has you dealing directly with animals, there are agencies you will want to check in with, even if certificates or their approval is not necessary. In the US, these are Animal Control and the Department of Health. Most pet industry businesses would be well advised to check in with their local Department of Agriculture, as well. Even pet supplies stores that may never have contact with their end consumers should stay in contact with the Department of Agriculture. All these agencies can provide information, guidelines, and relevant updates you may need for as long as your business is operational.

TAXPAYER ID

To collect and then pay taxes as a business, you will need to get an EIN (Employer Identification Number). For some businesses, your social security number (your personal taxpayer identification number) may be enough for your business obligations. Contact your local IRS or tax authority office (or go online) to fill out the necessary forms to create your business tax identity.

BUSINESS BANK ACCOUNTS

Business bank accounts are not the same as personal bank accounts. There are both benefits and obligations associated with business accounts that you will not have with your personal account. Opening a business bank account requires documentation that personal accounts do not require. Your bank manager will tell you which documents you must provide in order to open the various accounts you will need.

Not all banks are created equal. Shop around before deciding which bank is best suited to your business.

Chapter 5.

While it is possible to handle all your finances without ever having to step into a bank or speak directly with a human banker, this is not recommended as you establish yourself as a business owner. There may come a time that you will need human intervention or a face-to-face conversation with your bank representative. It is far better to have an established relationship with your bank's tellers and loan officers before you need to ask for a loan or ask to have a fee waived.

Keep your business accounts, debts, and revenues separate from your personal money. Never co-mingle personal and business money, ever.

What will you need from your bank?

CHECKING ACCOUNT
Get the most basic business account your bank offers. Most banks want your business and will offer deals for small business owners. If you have a partner, be sure they have access to this account, too.

BUSINESS CREDIT CARD
This is for purchases for the business only. Do not use it for personal purchases.

BANKING AND PAYMENT APPS
You need to set up banking and payment apps for your business. Do not use your personal banking apps, accounts, or credit cards for your business. It might be tempting to use a personal account to save on commissions or transaction fees. That is ill-advised. Besides raising red flags to tax authorities, financial app platforms are savvy and you could be red-flagged for abusing their systems.

There is an ever-growing list of banking and payment apps to choose from. Most are quite secure; some are extremely secure. None are impenetrable. Just as you would not leave your wallet lying around, protect your banking portals.

Check them daily and report any discrepancies immediately.

Which financial apps are best for you? There is no perfect answer; each business has its own unique set of criteria. Speak with sales and tech support from several financial apps. Explain what your needs are. Find the one that works best for you and costs as little as possible while providing the best, most secure service. After all your research, you might choose to use several payment apps simultaneously which would allow more payment, scheduling, or communication options for your clients. Just don't overdo it; you don't want to spend all your time online tracking payments.

When possible, try out free versions of all apps and software platforms you are interested in. Take time to check out their customer support before you completely commit to a particular service. Sooner or later almost all software needs support, and you definitely do not want to be left blowing in the wind if your payment app crashes.

Don't let your decision be completely based on fees. Yes, paying a percentage of each transaction adds up. But payment apps and online banking financial software should lessen the time you spend banking and collecting payments; and time is money. They can also ease the burden of record keeping if you choose apps that can be integrated into your bookkeeping system. And that is a savings, too. Except for depositing cash, all your finances should be able to be handled electronically.

A word about cash: if you accept cash payments be sure to 1) enter them immediately into your financial books and 2) deposit them as soon as possible to your business bank account. It is far too easy to accidentally mingle your personal cash with cash that belongs to your business. The former belongs to you, the latter belongs to your business.

By staying up-to-date with all your cash transactions, you will not find yourself owing taxes on money that never made it into your accounts. And you never want to find yourself having to explain to the IRS why there is no record of payment for services provided.

<u>LINE OF CREDIT</u>
While your credit is good, try to secure a credit line. You won't pay for it unless you need it. And when you need it, *if* you need it, it will be available.

<u>CREDIT CARD PROCESSOR</u>
If you intend to accept credit card payments for your products and services, you need to enroll with a company that will process these payments. Speak with your banker and see what the bank can offer. Then shop around and see if you can find a better deal with an independent credit card processor. Ask your bank to match it. If they cannot, go for the best credit card processing (with the best service) you can find.

That concludes the "must haves" for initially setting up a business. What else do new businesses need?

Once the legalities and financials are settled, to start off on the right foot with your new business, you will want to equip yourself with the tools you need to make your business run as smoothly and efficiently as possible. It takes more than a sturdy leash or a big backyard to properly run a pet care business.

TECHNOLOGY AS BUSINESS TOOLS
Business-oriented mobile or PC-based software applications can help your business, and your life, run more smoothly. Do an online search and ask around to see which apps are best suited for your business.

Some apps are free, some are not. Some offer free trial periods. While some apps and platforms charge per use, others charge you once to download, and never again.

Don't get sucked into what looks like a great deal but doesn't truly answer your needs. While there are exceptions to the rule, you will, more often than not, get what you pay for. Free may be appealing while you are facing so many other expenses; but the right software can be a game changer. Try to look ahead and imagine what you may need in the future. Choose the software that does the most for you today and that will continue to meet your needs for the long haul.

Besides the banking and payment apps already discussed, these are the types of software apps that will be most helpful to you:

- Networking
- Social media
- Scheduling
- Workforce management

Additionally, boarding and doggy daycare businesses should consider kennel management software. Alternatively, a retail store or manufacturing company will probably need software to track employee hours, manage logistics, or to coordinate group projects.

If you plan to run a network of subcontractors there are apps that will allow you to book, track, and pay those contractors 100% electronically.

For the purposes of this book, the terms mobile app and platform are used interchangeably, even though they are technologically different. Do not let the terminology get in your way. Unless you want to develop mobile apps for the pet industry, the differences are of no significance.

Chapter 5.

NETWORKING APPS

There are two types of networking apps for businesses. The first type is for professionals only, where people working in the field can share and vent with peers. Professional networking apps can be very good sources of information and a way to keep up to date with what is going on in your region and in the industry as a whole. Don't be a taker; give and share as much as you glean.

The second type of networking apps includes those that are open to the public. This is where your potential customers can find and connect with you. Some will allow your clients to seamlessly book your services.

Public networking platforms that offer a booking function will almost always have a fee attached to it; that is how the app developer maintains the platform and makes money. Do not dismiss these out of hand just because of the fee. Instead, consider the reach of those apps and factor those fees into your cost of doing business. Compare the cost of the app with the cost to hire someone to answer the phone and book appointments 24 hours a day.

Some pet owners prefer to hire through these apps because they believe it increases the chances they are hiring someone reliable and safe, and that their payment is better protected.

The two major downsides to these apps are the fees (when they occur) and the data farming that goes on behind the scenes. Only you can decide whether or not data farming is something you can live with.

Find and use apps, particularly the public ones, with strong administrators and rules of use. These apps can be good avenues for marketing and advertising, but they can also open a can of worms in the form of public negative feedback or reviews. You should be judicious about what you post on them. Do not post photos of your clients' pets without their permission. Never post photos of your clients' homes. Avoid posting anything negative about your competition, or clients, even if you do not refer to them by name. Be positive. If you are the target of negative posts, contact the administrator immediately.

SOCIAL MEDIA PLATFORMS

There are dozens of social media platforms to choose from. Facebook, Twitter, Instagram, and TikTok are the most famous and prolific, but there are others in the market. Different audiences prefer different platforms so be prepared to use more than one. See which are the best matches for you.

Be consistent in your tone and content. You are not only communicating and booking business through social media, you are building a brand. Be sure *all* your content reflects your business' brand. It is vital that you are aware of, and in control of, how you are projecting and protecting your brand on social media at all times. What you post and how you post it can make or break your business. Be careful not to expose yourself to legal jeopardy by posting anything you may come to regret. Do not post in anger. Do not share content or photos you do not have permission to post. Be honest but selective. Post regularly, but more important than quantity, is quality. Your goal should be to engage a following that will drive business to you.

If you are unsure about what and how to post or how to best use social media, speak with an expert. You may find an "expert" among the teens and 20-something-year-olds you know who have been raised with social media and who, for a few dollars, or a gift card to their favorite store, will help guide you until you are more confident in utilizing this media. Of course, you could always hire them (or a seasoned professional social media manager) to do this work for you. But remember, it is your business, your brand, your name that is on the line. Oversight is crucial.

WEBSITE

There are potential clients who will not even consider you or your services if they cannot find you easily on the web. Some of that has to do with convenience and some of that comes down to perceived legitimacy. They want to be sure you are running a legitimate business. They may want to read reviews about you before they contact you. And, quite honestly, some want to see if you have made the effort and investment in reaching them before they make the effort to reach or hire you.

Do not underestimate the worth of a good website. It may be old-school technologically speaking, but websites are a great avenue to get your business known and drive business to you.

If you can afford to, hire an experienced website developer. If the money for that is not available early on, launch a website yourself. There are many platforms on which even the least tech-savvy business owner can create their own basic website. Keep it simple. When you can afford to, if you feel you must, pay a professional to upgrade it.

Regardless of who builds it, do not use content or photos that you do not own or have not paid a licensing fee for. Make sure your contact information is correct and up-to-date. From time-to-time make sure the website is live and working properly.

SCHEDULING APPS

Scheduling apps come in all shapes and sizes. Some are as simple as a calendar where you manually fill in the appointments and commitments for each day. Some are far more complex allowing clients to self-book and send out automated reminder emails.

Do your homework to find the scheduling software that answers your needs and is an asset, not a source of stress.

THE HUMAN RESOURCES OF YOUR BUSINESS

All the tools and tech resources in the world cannot replace a well-trained, enthusiastic staff.

Hopefully, there will come a time when your business will be successful enough to hire employees or subcontractors to work for, or expand, your business. Some staff will be support personnel doing the back of house tasks such as bookkeeping or scheduling. Others may be providing services directly to your clients and customers. No matter what the position, hiring people should never be taken lightly.

You may not be able to afford to hire staff right away, but you should plan for that day. Now is the time to think about what positions you will want to fill and what makes your ideal employee a good match for you. You should also have a plan for taking care of all those who work for you. Once hired, your employees will rely on the income they receive from you. Be sure you can afford your employees before you commit to them. Laying off employees should be a last resort. So should firing them.

It is your responsibility to train your employees. Even if they are experienced in their field, if you want them to do things your way, you need to show them what your way looks like. They aren't mind readers.

It will also be your responsibility to ensure they are respected and protected from customers and other employees. Develop procedures and protocols. Write a formal employee handbook. Research what the law says and take a look around and see what employees expect. Then do better than the minimum.

Chapter 5.

Research wages in your area and in your industry. Plan on paying your team as much as you can, not as little as you can get away with; this is not the place to save a few pennies. If you want to attract the best employees pay more than your competitors pay.

How will you know it is time to look for employees, contractors, or third-party service providers? Refer back to your checklist of daily, weekly, and monthly tasks that your business requires. If all the action items are done properly and on time, you are probably fine. When you start to fall behind in completing your to-do list, it will be time to consider hiring help.

Depending on your business type and the size and scope of that business, some staff may be employees and some may be subcontractors. Some of your team may be outside contractors and others will be service providers.

There are different working constructs, and they require different recordkeeping and different documentation. As you did your market research in anticipation of writing your business plan, hopefully you considered how you want to structure your business in terms of staffing. If you did not, go back and do that now.

EMPLOYEES
Hiring employees can be both a blessing and a burden. Many new business owners find this one of the most stressful aspects of running a business. It certainly brings with it a lot of responsibility. Choose well and then take good care of them.

Taking care of employees is not just paying their taxes and unemployment insurance properly (though you absolutely need to do those!). It means:

- Making sure they are trained properly before you expect them to work independently.

- Respecting them by fixing a schedule and not changing it on a whim.

- Providing a safe work environment.

- Taking the time to create a well-thought-out and thorough employee's manual. Create and write down protocols and procedures that work for you and protect them.

Where can you find employees? In a word, everywhere. That friendly bagger at your grocery store might be looking for a better job or even a career. Your friends might know of people who are looking to get into pet care. School bulletin boards are great places to post if you are looking for parttime staff. Consider using a placement (staffing) service. These companies have huge databases of potential employees and may run the payroll of your new hires, which can be beneficial to you as you are busy scaling up. It can save you the headache of adding and deleting employees to your payroll during their trial employment period. This savings alone can justify any fees you pay to the staffing service

CONTRACTORS, SUBCONTRACTORS, AND BUSINESS SERVICES PROVIDERS
Whether or not you decide to hire employees, there may be tasks from your to-do list that are better handled by third-party service providers.

SERVICE PROVIDERS
These are the people whose work supports your business without being a part of your business. You will almost certainly not be their only client. They will bill you for their time and you will pay them against a periodic invoice.

In business, often the first task that is delegated to a third-party provider is tax preparation. In theory you could manage all your taxes yourself, but it will take you longer than a CPA and since you are not a tax expert, you run the risk of overlooking some deduction or obligation, neither of which you want to do.

Bookkeeping, even with the help of bookkeeping software, is often the second task delegated to an outsider. If bookkeeping is taking up time that could better be used for actually generating income, hiring a bookkeeper can be a wise investment. Find someone who is not only accurate but trustworthy. Then check their work, at least at the beginning of your relationship.

Other service providers may include, depending on your specific business: A live or virtual assistant, PR firm, logistics, warehouse management, or shippers. Hiring a third party cleaning service, or landscapers can free up your time to generate far more income than those services cost.

SUBCONTRACTORS ARE LIKE EMPLOYEES BUT LEGALLY DIFFERENT

Subcontractors provide the services you advertise under your banner but are not *legally* your employees. These are people who work in your business but manage their own taxes. You will need to provide them with a tax accounting form at the end of each fiscal year (this is a 1099 in the US). You do not pay their taxes for them. They prepare, file, and pay their own taxes. They may work for you full- or part-time; they may or may not work for you exclusively.

While they may be legally independent, subcontractors represent you and your business. Your clients and customers do not know who is an independent contractor or whose taxes you pay. For many of your customers, they are simply the face of your business. Evaluate, interview, and hire them at least as cautiously as you would an employee. Be clear in the expectations and obligations each party is bringing to the arrangement.

Finally, regarding your investment in human resources, invest in learning how to be a good boss so people will want to work for you. If you get a reputation as a bad boss you will see applications dry up. Learn from the businesses around you (both the successful ones and those that failed) and learn from those businesses and organizations for which you have worked. Ask yourself, "What was management like?" "What did they do right and what did they do badly?"

If you are a good boss, the likelihood of your employees doing the best job for you is greater and they will stay with you longer. Less turnover saves you time and money. But even the best bosses lose employees from time-to-time. Account for employee turnover.

BITS AND PIECES FOR STARTING ANY BUSINESS

- Protect yourself and your investment. Get the proper insurance for your business and be sure to get enough of it.

- Protect your business. Always be in compliance with any and all regulations.

- Know your limitations and stick to your guns. Do not grow your business faster than you can manage.

- Your employees reflect you and your business. They may be the first, if not the only, face your clients or customers encounter. Choose them wisely.

- Use all technology carefully. Protect passwords and use firewalls.

- Be judicious in what you post on social media. If it is something you would not say in public, you should not put it in a post.

- Be prepared for crises.

- Remember that this is a business. Act like it at all times.

It's finally time to take a look at what it takes to succeed in your chosen pet industry niche. Ready?

The following chapters discuss in detail the formation and running of eleven different pet industry businesses. As they all exist within the same industry, some recommendations and action items may overlap. As you read through them all, some information may feel repetitive. Consider the context before you dismiss it as redundant.

However tempting it is to skip chapters, it's recommended that you read each chapter and familiarize yourself with the wide variety of pet industry businesses, regardless of the specific business you are focusing on. There is something to be learned from each chapter and from each business.

Besides, you never know when opportunity may come knocking from a complementary business sometime in the future.

Chapter 6.
SETTING UP A PET SITTING BUSINESS

Flexibility: Moderate to high

Investment level: Very low

Startup costs: $0-$50/month

Mandatory education: None

Recommended education: Pet CPR, pet behavior classes, basic bookkeeping

Necessary equipment: Smartphone

Recommended equipment: Designated keys organizer, registration on one or more industry mobile app, business cards, electronic payment & receipt apps, website (multilingual if you plan to work internationally), social media accounts, accounts on booking platforms, passport (if you plan to work internationally)

Legal requirements: For each jurisdiction in which you accept work, you may be required to register as a business and set up accounts for paying local (as well as federal) taxes; insurance; if you work internationally, you will need a passport and you must check and comply with local work permit requirements.

WHY DO PEOPLE HIRE PET SITTERS?
There are many reasons a pet owner may hire a pet sitter: vacation travel, business travel, family emergency travel, or any number of disturbances in their everyday life such as illness. Regardless of the "why," your job as a pet sitter is to care for their pets at the same level of care your client provides, if not better.

Pet sitting brings with it enormous responsibilities. Your clients are relying on your dedication and good judgment. They are entrusting you with their beloved pets while they are away or indisposed and possibly unreachable.

While all pet care relationships are built on trust, the level of trust a client places in a pet sitter is multi-fold. Not only are they entrusting their companions to your care, but they are also opening their home to you. They are trusting you not only to be honest but to be discreet. They are counting on your common sense and stability as well as your reliability and expertise. And, at least initially, they will be somewhat relying on blind faith. Earn that faith and their trust.

Be respectful and understanding of all their concerns and fears. With luck and hard work, you can build up a repeat-client list which will allow you to get to know their pets and their household routines. This will make each subsequent engagement that much easier.

It is particularly important that before you offer your services, you have a clear vision of what you mean when you say pet sitter and what services you will offer. Think about what it is you want to do, what you are willing to do, and what you will not agree to do as part of your service.

WHAT DO PET SITTERS DO?
Pet sitting comes in many shapes and sizes. Some pet sitters will work several sitting jobs at once. They may limit their obligation to feeding the cat and cleaning the litter box. They might take a dog out a few times a day and feed them but will not spend all their time with one specific family and they may not stay overnight.

Other pet sitters commit to a single family at a time. These pet sitters may go to a day job and, like the pets' owners, they care for household pets before and after work. In some cases, at night the pet sitter goes home to sleep; in others, the sitter stays over.

Still other sitters will move in as part of the contract. Caring for their clients' home and all the pets in it is their full-time job. Every aspect of the pets' care is the sitter's responsibility. The sitter may also agree to bring in the mail, water the plants, and generally let the world know that the house is occupied.

Most international pet sitting opportunities work this overnight/extended contract model. In fact, many pet sitters use these opportunities to travel and experience new places up close and live almost like the locals. Once the pets in their care are seen to in the morning, these sitters explore the local sites, returning home only when it's walking- or feeding-time or at the end of the day to care for the pets and then to sleep.

Pet sitting jobs can be contracted for a number of days or a number of weeks.

There is no right or wrong way to model your pet sitting business. Pet sitting is incredibly flexible and you can mix and match contracts to suit your needs.

Set your own parameters. Price accordingly.

PARAMETERS FOR PET SITTING BUSINESSES
Since there are different models on which to build your pet sitting business and since the term Pet Sitter can mean different things to different people, you need to be clear what your services include and what they do not.

WHAT TYPES OF ANIMALS WILL YOU, CAN YOU, WORK WITH?
This is a really important key question you need to ask yourself. Dogs and cats are not the only pets you could be asked to care for. Do you have an affinity for (and experience) caring for birds or exotic animals? Bird sitting

could be your niche market. So could caring for lizards if you have the expertise. On the other hand, if you do not like birds or lizards (or are scared of them) you can exclude those pets from your list of care recipients. There is no need to advertise "not" caring for birds; simply do not add them to your list of services. Try to be positive in turning down those jobs which are not in your wheelhouse. There really is no need to share your dislike or fear of birds (or lizards); you can simply say that you lack the knowledge and experience needed to work with those animals and leave it at that.

But should a potential client insist, be honest, open, and firm about your limitations. Do not let a client talk you into caring for an animal you are not comfortable caring for.

Price your services properly. The fewer pet sitters there are, the more you can charge for caring for them. If you focus on more common domestic pets, check the going rates among your competitors and set your rates accordingly. If you can care for less common domestic pets or exotic animals, which few sitters can or will, be sure to price your services to reflect that.

FULL-TIME OR PART-TIME?
Will this be your full-time job or is this business a supplemental income? If it is supplemental, consider the entire time commitment you will be making to care for the pets you have been hired to care for, including the time spent on commuting to and from each client. Can you afford to take time off from your day job to tend to a sick pet in your care? What if there is a different type of emergency? Will you be able to deal with emergencies if you have other obligations?

Be honest and upfront with your clients as to when you will be caring for their pets and when you will *not* be there. Since most people do spend some part of their day away from home and away from their pets, many clients are fine with the fact that you will not be available 24/7 as long as you do show up and care for their pets exactly as promised, if not more. Othe clients want you available 24/7 for the duration of the contract. Don't agree to any terms you are not comfortable with.

<u>MOVE IN OR SLEEP AT HOME</u>
Pet sitting done locally might allow you to return to your own home at the end of the day. In fact, it is possible to pet sit for several clients at once if they are all local and all require only a visit or two each day.

If your services include staying overnight at your client's home, you still may be able to take on other work or work your regular 9-to-5 job.

Offering to stay overnight can be a premium service for which you can charge a premium fee. For that premium fee, your client may expect more of your undivided attention and more obligations (i.e. water the plants, take in the mail). Be specific about what your services include. Be specific about what your clients' obligations are as well.

Are they providing meals for your overnight stays? Are you invited to drink their liquor? Will you be permitted to access their WiFi? Will you be permitted to use their car?

Be sure to detail your obligations as well as theirs and include them in your contract.

<u>SET GEOGRAPHIC BOUNDARIES</u>
How far are you willing to travel?

You could limit yourself to sitting for pets only in the high-rise apartment building where you live. Alternatively, you could expand your reach and take on clients within a 5-, 10-, or 20-mile radius from your home. You could set your boundaries to a few states abutting your own. Or, if you choose to use this business to feed your wanderlust, you can offer your services internationally!

When setting your rates, take into account the time and distance needed to reach your clients. You can fold these into a higher base rate or you could require a per mile/per trip travel fee.

Be sure your schedule includes the time it takes to travel to each client. If you don't, and you take on more than one client at a time, you might find yourself greatly over-extended (and not complying with your agreement) if you are stuck in traffic or are facing a bus strike.

Working internationally can be great and exciting but it does come with its own set of challenges. Since each job is relatively short-lived, most countries will not require you to register as a business entity or pay local taxes; *but they could*. Some countries require visas just to enter and their laws may greatly restrict your ability to work, even as a pet sitter.

If you are considering international pet sitting, or pet sitting across state borders, remember that travel plans get interrupted all too often, so you might have a booking that gets cancelled at the last moment or your flights can be delayed.

Working internationally, or even just across state lines, may require additional attention to bookkeeping and paying proper taxes in multiple jurisdictions.

This is not to put you off international or distance pet sitting. It is to say that thought, planning, and attention need to be given to it.

THE JOB OF PET SITTING
Depending on the pet you are caring for, pet sitting may include:

- Taking pets on walks or providing other exercise
- Playing and interacting with the pet(s) in your care
- Feeding the pet(s) correctly and on time
- Providing water
- Brushing or light grooming
- Shopping for pet food
- Dispensing medications
- Handling veterinarian emergencies
- Doing light housekeeping
- Starting the car from time-to-time
- Taking phone messages
- Being a presence in the house against burglars
- Watering plants or bringing in the mail
- And so on..

When setting up your pet sitting business, decide which services you are willing, able, and qualified to provide. Consider which you want to include in your basic pet sitting package and which services you will offer as add-ons for additional fees. Be open to adding services you hadn't thought of before. Add or delete services you enjoy or dislike.

MARKETING YOUR PET SITTING BUSINESS
How you market your pet sitting business will depend on where your territory is. If you decide that you only want to work within walking distance from your apartment, you might be able to get by with a few local flyers and joining a neighborhood social media chat group. Local vet offices may allow you to put a stack of flyers or business cards on their counters.

If you want to extend your reach, join additional social media groups and network among regional face-to-face networking or social groups. It's recommended that you launch a website and you do need a social media presence, no matter how small your target area is.

As was discussed in previous chapters, a simple, but attractive and informative website can make all the difference when you are first setting out. Even a basic landing page can be helpful. It doesn't have to be fancy or complex. But it does need to be thoughtful, attractive, and maintained. If you aim to reach further, a more developed website is a must.

Along with your website, sign up for a reliable video-conferencing service. You may get to know your clients near your home before beginning your sitting job, but it is not uncommon for pet sitters who work internationally, or even just regionally, to never meet their clients in real life. Having a video chat or two will allow clients to get to know you, even if you never meet face-to-face. This not only adds legitimacy and professionalism to your business, this gives *you* an opportunity to check out the client and possibly the client's pet and home before you commit to them.

Even if you are only focusing on clients in your immediate vicinity, get active on social media. Potential clients will want to know as much as possible about you before they hire you and allow you into their home.

As you post to social media, you must be extremely careful not to share anything about a client's home or their private details. With permission, many pet owners are fine with their sitters posting cute videos of their pets. Always get permission first. Never disclose pets' names. Do not post in real time (this could let thieves know the homeowners are away). Be discrete and do not post any information that would disclose your clients' names or address.

Chapter 6.

If you are unable to post about your interactions with your clients' pets, you can still use social media to your advantage. Tell tales and short stories of your adventures. Just be sure to change all the names and anything that could identify your clients.

In the early days following the launch of your business, you might want to invest in advertising your services. Consider taking limited ad space on those digital platforms as well as in any local newspapers in the areas you are targeting. Using local or mass media to advertise does not necessarily mean big advertising budgets. There are ways to utilize media to promote yourself without paying for targeted advertising.

Contact local news agencies wherever you work or want to work. Write them a smashing press release in which you talk about yourself and your business and offer to be on their newscast to talk about you, your services, and your expertise. This can be done in studio or remotely. Getting interviewed costs you nothing but your time.

Other ways to advertise your new pet sitting business is through booking apps for pet sitters. Even though they may charge you a service fee that comes out of your income, do not overlook booking services (online and mobile based) where clients are looking for the very services you provide. These apps are relatively inexpensive for the business owner. Some charge a small monthly fee while others charge you only when you book clients by taking a percentage of the booking.

In exchange for these fees, the more advanced pet care apps can collect payment on your behalf, connect clients with your pre-written contract (or provide a standard contract), and may even eliminate the need to maintain more than a basic website. Most of them allow you to write a bio that clients can check out before contacting you, saving precious time.

These platforms can provide a level of protection for you (and your clients) since there is an onboarding process that can be verified before acceptance. This can be particularly helpful - and worth every cent - if you intend to work overseas or far from home with no other way to check out who the clients are or what you are walking into.

Choose the marketing platform and campaign that best suit the parameters you have set for yourself.

MANAGING YOUR PET SITTING BUSINESS

As is true for all businesses, before you start pet sitting, you need to establish a business entity and all that is associated with a new business. This will not only give a "professional face" to what you do, it will allow you to keep your business and personal finances separate. It also provides you with a clear mechanism for paying taxes. And a proper business entity protects you and your personal assets since they are not part of your business.

Once legally and financially established, what do you need to run your pet sitting business?

TECH FOR PET SITTERS

Invest in the best mobile phone and pay for the best internet service you can afford. These are your business' lifelines. Your phone is your office. Back it up regularly or work entirely in the cloud so your data is protected from accidental loss.

If you can afford to, buy a second phone or at the very least, pay for a second line on a single phone (make sure your phone is either dual SIM or can accept an eSIM). Use one for your business and one for your personal use. This provides a barrier between the two worlds: your business and your private life.

Create a short, pleasant welcoming message for your business voicemail and set up an automatic reply. For all your social media chats and your email, do the same.

Since much of your day you might be busy with caring for clients and their pets, or possibly working a full-time job outside of pet sitting, you should let callers know that their call is important and that you will get back to them later. Be sure to return their calls as soon as you can. Set aside time every day to return phone calls and emails.

As you read earlier, you will need a social media presence and you will need a website. Without one, there will be clients that will not even consider you and will move on to the next pet sitter. Even if most of your clients come through booking apps, you do not want to miss any potential clients who first want to learn something about you before they call or book. Make sure the mobile version of your site looks as good as the desktop version.

Engage followers on social media. Engage, even if you do not share new content, every day. There is no need to overshare and you should never share anything personal or revealing about any of your clients or their pets. If you intend to use photos of your clients' pets on social media, get a signed release first.

Upload and activate several payment apps. Even if you plan to use a third-party booking service that will collect your fees, be ready to make and receive business transactions with your own financial accounts.

RECORDKEEPING

Keep accurate records, particularly if you are not using an online booking service or if you receive any cash payments.

Recordkeeping is especially important if you work across tax jurisdictions. Your good recordkeeping will ensure you pay all your taxes but that you do not overpay.

If your income is routed through a third-party booker or app, each transaction will be recorded and you will be able to access those records at the end of each day, each month, or each fiscal quarter. Some platforms will deal with any taxes you need to pay and provide you with a record of them being paid, saving you the headache. Most third-party bookers will not pay your taxes but will provide you with the appropriate forms and information so that you can report and pay your taxes accurately.

Be sure to check booking reports regularly to make sure they are accurate and that you catch any mistakes immediately. And it never hurts to keep your own records and compare them with the reports generated by your third-party bookers.

Besides tracking payments for taxes, you should keep accurate and detailed records of your work day.

- Your record keeping should include chronicling all your activities so that at the end of the day your clients know what you did and when you did it. A short summary is all it takes to keep your clients informed and to protect yourself against any false accusations.

- Record as much information as possible about the pets you will be caring for when you are hired. Don't assume you will remember everything. You won't. Include food and feeding instructions; meds and dispensing schedules; grooming needs; rules of the house; quirks of each pet. Then record when you completed or noted each of these.

Chapter 6.

An alternative to having to write a detailed narrative for each client is to create a checklist and calendar to use for each job. Each time you perform that service, check it off, date and time stamp it, and initial it. Then share that with your client.

<u>SETTING YOUR FEES</u>
When first starting out you may not know how much to charge for your services. Look around and see what your competitors are charging. Then decide where you want to be relative to them.

You may choose to be the premier sitter in your area and you will set your fees high. Or you may choose to set your fees just slightly below the most expensive sitter in town. This gives clients a sense that they are getting a deal.

You could try to undercut all your competition by charging less in hopes of bringing clients unhappy with paying top dollar. That can work, but you run the risk of giving potential clients the impression that you are the discount provider in terms of quality, not just price. It may invite only bargain hunters and not long-term clients willing to pay for great service.

Only you can decide where to position your business. Just consider long-term implications, not just short-term needs, before you position yourself and set your fees.

You have many options for how to determine your fees and rates for your menu of services. You could set fees based on an à la carte menu of what jobs you are willing to do and how often you do them. Each task has a price and each client chooses which tasks they are willing to pay you to do.

Alternatively, you could charge for each visit over the course of the day. Or you could charge a flat day- or weekly- rate. A single outing per day may have one fee, but multiple walks may come with a discount.

Or you can create a hybrid menu of basic services with add-ons. Your daily flat rate may include a set of basic tasks and then additional add-ons cost more.

Possible add-ons or upcharges could include:

- Dispensing medications
- Cleaning the kitty litter box
- Additional walks
- Additional pets
- Light grooming or nail trims
- Arranging or transporting to scheduled vet or grooming visits
- Emergency vet transportation

If you are hired for a job far from home, will you require/set a fee for compensation for travel time or expenses, or will that be rolled into one set fee? Or do you want to stick with your standard day (or per visit) rate and add a per-mile transportation fee?

There are no right or wrong answers for setting fees and price structuring. With experience and as your business grows, you will almost certainly, from time to time, change your fees and fee structures. The more in demand you are, the higher your fees can be.

INSURANCE

Get insurance. Get as much as you can afford. This is not an area to cut costs. Speak with an insurance agent with experience insuring pet sitters and get as much and as broad coverage as is necessary to protect yourself and your assets.

Chapter 6.

CONTRACTS

Pet sitters need a rock-solid contract. Your contract, alongside your insurance, is there to protect you. It should clearly explain which services you are providing and what your fees are. It should also delineate those things that are *not* your responsibility.

This contract is not to be taken lightly and it is beyond worth the money you may pay to have a licensed attorney draw one up.

If you choose to work through a booking service, read their contract carefully and learn every detail it spells out. If it doesn't cover everything you want, maybe that booking service isn't for you.

EXPANDING YOUR PET SITTING BUSINESS

Of all the pet care businesses, pet sitting might be the most difficult of all to scale up. So much of the business is simply you: your knowledge, experience, character, and reputation; even your personality. And of course, there is the fact that you can only be in one place (one client's home) at any one time. Yet, there are a few ways to scale up, expand business, and add revenue streams for pet sitters.

One option is to create a pet sitting referral service or platform. Even though there are a few already in play, nothing is stopping you from creating your own networking/booking service where pet sitters and clients can come together. As such a business grows, you might find yourself having to step away from actual pet sitting in order to maintain this business.

Another option is to take on carefully screened employees. They can be either true employees or subcontractors. In either case you would not only have to vet them to the nth degree, but you would need to train them to your satisfaction and constantly monitor them. This is not for the faint of heart. The risks are high and the perils many. But if done well, employees could allow you to have an income whether you are available for pet sitting or not. It can expand your reach. And it can allow you to build a business beyond yourself while still allowing you to do what you love to do: take care of pets.

ADDITIONAL REVENUE STREAMS

Pet sitters may find themselves with time between gigs. You can use that time to create additional revenue streams that will not interfere with your pet sitting business. In fact, many can complement your primary business of pet sitting.

Some additional revenue streams you might want to consider are:

ONLINE RETAIL

If you have an internet connection, you can start an online retail store. Running an online store is something you can do during your down time or even while you pet sit, especially if you use drop-shipping instead of holding inventory that you would need to package and ship yourself.

WRITE

Of course, you would not be required to write about pets or animals, but what a great opportunity you will have to do so! You could write about the pets you care for, or your adventures along the way.

PET TRANSPORTATION

What a great way to maximize your travel time to pet sitting jobs! Professional pet transportation is a business unto itself, but there is no reason you cannot transport a pet occasionally and charge for it.

Chapter 6.

Contact pet rescues in your area. If they have animals heading in the same direction you are, offer to either drive them or accompany them on planes. This may or may not get you an income, but the rescue may pay for your gas or flight.

Be sure to read Chapter 10 to learn how to create a Pet Transportation company properly and effectively.

BITS AND PIECES FOR PET SITTERS
- Get insurance and be bonded. Be sure your coverage includes all your intended jurisdictions.

- Keep a detailed record of all you do for pets in your care and do this for each visit/contract. Take lots of photos for the record and share them with your client along with your documentation of events and activities.

- Make sure *their* home insurance covers *you* while in their home.

- Be sure you have a backup plan in case you need to cancel. Go the extra mile plus not to cancel, but if you have to cancel, don't leave your clients hanging.
- Get emergency contacts from your clients. You do not want to find yourself pet sitting an animal whose owner's return is delayed to the point that it interferes with your next job, or whose owner never returns. Get multiple emergency contacts and always have a Plan B backup plan. And a Plan C.

- Address language barriers, particularly if you choose to work internationally. NOT EVERYONE SPEAKS ENGLISH! Learn a few key words in the local language before you arrive. If your client is struggling in English either try to find a common language you both know or use a digital translator.

It may not be a great translation, but it is typically good enough to get the message across.

- Invest in a reliable smartphone. It is your lifeline to your clients, emergency services, and home. It is your camera, your tape recorder, your file cabinet, and your connection to social media and future clients.

- Make sure the pet owners have a credit card on file with their vet just in case any of the pets you are caring for need medical care.

- Get a deposit and if possible, get paid in advance. At the very least, have a non-refundable cancellation charge and make sure that payment is made before you turn down other work.

Chapter 7.
LAUNCHING A PROFESSIONAL DOG WALKING BUSINESS

Flexibility: High

Investment level: Very low

Startup costs: As little as $0 up to $50 a month for phone and website

Mandatory education: None

Recommended education: Pet CPR, pet behavior classes, basic bookkeeping

Necessary equipment: None

Recommended equipment: Couplers, quality leashes, keys organizer, tablet and/or smart-phone, registration on industry mobile app(s), business cards, electronic payment & receipt app(s), basic website

Legal requirements: Some jurisdictions require you to register as a business and set up accounts for paying taxes and insurance

WHY DO PEOPLE HIRE DOG WALKERS?
It is really quite simple: Dog walkers ensure dogs get walked when the owners are unable to walk them. But why? And how?

There are a multitude of reasons a dog owner cannot walk their own dogs and instead, hire a dog walker. It is not just people being lazy.

Sometimes hiring a dog walker is a solution to a temporary problem. Perhaps the owner is incapacitated through illness or injury. During the time of COVID-19, for instance, humans restricted to isolation still needed their dogs taken out for exercise or potty.

There are those who hire dog walkers for the early months of their dog's life when the puppy needs to be taken out frequently, but the owner cannot be home during the day.

Some clients need to be out of town for a short stay but do not want to, or cannot, take their dog to a boarding kennel. There are times and circumstances when a dog walker is a better solution than a boarding kennel.

In all these cases, and others, hiring a dog walker is an excellent solution to a short-term dilemma.

Additionally, some dog owners hire dog walkers as permanent service providers for their dog. These might be people working long hours who do not want their dogs cooped up at home all day. Or dog walkers may be hired to ensure a dog gets more exercise than the owner is able to provide.

Some owners want their solo dogs to have some exposure to other dogs and hire a dog walker who will take their pup out in a pack, a group.

The reasons are many and varied. As a business owner, you would be wise not to judge the reason the dog's owner needs help caring for their dog. Focus on the dog and the great service you are providing for them.

ESTABLISHING YOUR DOG WALKING BUSINESS
Dog Walking is very similar to Pet Sitting in how it needs to be set up as a business and managed.

<u>CREATE A BUSINESS ENTITY</u>
Before you start walking other people's dogs professionally (that is, for pay), you should establish a business entity and all that is associated with your new

business such as bank accounts. This will not only give a "professional face" to what you do, it will allow you to keep your business and personal finances separate. It also provides you a clear, legal mechanism for accepting payments and paying expenses. And setting up a business properly protects you and your personal assets.

- Set up your business as an entity that works best for you. This is likely an LLC. But it could be an S-Corp. Consult with an attorney or your state officials governing businesses and ask which entity works best for you in your jurisdiction.
- Register your business with the proper authorities.
- Set up your business' bank accounts.
- Get properly and sufficiently insured.

Once set up, what do you need to run your dog walking business?

YOUR PHONE, YOUR OFFICE

Invest in the best mobile phone and pay for the best internet service you can afford because for a dog walker, your phone is your office. Back it up regularly, or better yet, work entirely in the cloud so your data is protected from accidental loss.

If you can afford to, buy a second phone. At the very least, get a second phone number if you have a dual-SIM phone. Use one for your business and one for your personal use. This provides a barrier between the two worlds.

Create a short, pleasant welcoming message for your voicemail. You should let callers know that your hands may be full (literally) at the moment, but that their call is important and that you will get back to them as soon as possible.

There is more about using your phone for your Dog Walking business later in this chapter.

WEB PRESENCE, SOCIAL MEDIA, AND TECH

You will need a social media presence and you will need a website. Just as for pet sitters, potential customers expect to be able to find you and your business when searching for a dog walker. This is true even if most of your clients eventually come through booking apps.

Keep your website simple and from time-to-time check that it's working properly. Periodically, update it and change the content to keep it interesting and engaging.

It might actually be difficult for you to get good social media photos or videos because your hands will be busy handling leashes. Do your best to engage on social media regularly.

Other tech products and service you should consider using are:

- Self-booking apps
- Payment Apps with customizable invoicing, record keeping, and tax calculating functions
- Video Conferencing
- Online booking services

RECORDKEEPING

Keep accurate records, particularly if you are not using an online booking service or if you receive any cash payments.

If your income is routed through a third-party booker or app, each transaction will be recorded and you will be able to access those records at the end of each day, each month, or each fiscal quarter. Some platforms may deal with any taxes you need to pay and provide you with a record of them being paid, saving you the headache. Be sure to check these regularly to make sure they are accurate and that you catch any mistakes immediately. And it never hurts to keep your own records and compare them with third party bookers.

From day one, besides tracking payments and taxes you should get in the habit of keeping accurate and detailed records. These can be stored electronically, just be sure to back them up regularly.

Your recordkeeping should go beyond just revenue and taxes. It should include chronicling all your activities so that at the end of the day, your clients know what you did and when you did it. Create a short summary of each dog you walk each day to share with each appropriate client.

A short summary is all it takes to keep your clients informed and to protect yourself against any misunderstandings. Include when you arrived to pick up their dog and when you returned. Let your clients know about anything of concern that happened during the walk (loose stools, dog limping) and if you have time, let them know of any unusual (or perhaps amusing) incidents that might have occurred. Keeping them informed shows you are paying attention and clients appreciate that. Even if your client is home when you return from the walk, send them this document.

INSURANCE
Get insurance. Get as much and as comprehensive a policy as you can afford and one that protects you and your assets. Speak with an insurance agent with experience in this area to be sure you are insured for all possible scenarios.

CONTRACTS
Your contract, alongside your insurance, is there to protect you. It should clearly explain which services you are providing and what your fees are. Of no less importance is

to delineate where your responsibility and liability begin and end.

This contract is not to be taken lightly and may prove to be well worth the money you will pay to have a licensed attorney draw one up for you. If you choose to work through a booking service, read their contract carefully. If you are not happy with their contract or feel it does not protect you adequately, either use one of your own, or find a different booking service.

WHAT IT TAKES TO BE A PROFESSIONAL DOG WALKER

In theory, anyone can walk a dog. A 10-year-old can walk a dog. 85-year-olds walk dogs. But to be a *professional* dog walker, where clients will pay you to do this relatively simple, but necessary chore, entails much more than grabbing a leash and strolling around the block.

You must be able to identify and assess dangers, both obvious and lurking. You must remain vigilant and alert to them at all times.

You need to use good judgement at all times. Taking a young pup on a mile-long trek without a supply of water is simply dangerous. You, as the professional, would never do that. Not seeing a dog charging toward the dog you are walking as anything other than a potential threat is negligence. You, as the professional, would immediately recognize the risk and take evasive action.

Walking more than one dog at a time when one of those dogs has been identified as dog-aggressive, borders on the criminally negligent and this is something no professional would do. Even something as forgetting to bring poop-bags or allowing yourself to be distracted by a phone call while on the job, marks the difference between professional and unprofessional behavior.

Chapter 7.

You should be able to assess the general health of a dog. It does not take a degree in veterinary medicine to notice that a dog is limping, or has an upset stomach, or simply does not look well. Professional dog walkers will see these things immediately and take the proper action.

You must have the physical stamina dog walking requires, as well as the mental concentration. When you are walking dogs for clients you are not out for a stroll. You are working and you are responsible for those dogs from the moment they step outside their home until the moment they are safely back home.

Being a professional dog walker also necessitates you understand and internalize what dog owners choose service providers based on.

TRUST
It is essential that your clients trust you. You are taking their dog out of a safe environment, their home, into the streets or fields where all manner of dangers exists. That takes trust.

You may also be entering their homes unsupervised. Clients need to trust you to not disturb or damage their possessions and not abuse that access.

HONESTY
In some cases, dog walkers have unlimited access to their clients' homes. By entrusting you with a key (or passcode) to their home, your clients are relying on your honesty. Do not abuse it.

Do not bring your friends with you into clients' homes. Do not touch your clients' property. Touch nothing, take nothing. Not even a bottle of water from the fridge! If you are thirsty, take water from the tap (and let your client know you used a glass). Do not make yourself at home and watch TV, even while you are refilling water dishes.

RESPONSIBILITY

You are solely and completely responsible for everything that happens to their dog from the moment you enter their home until after you leave post-walk. That means making sure the dog (or any other pet) does not escape when you open the door. There is no "I've lost the key" or "I couldn't find your dog's leash." There is no "I thought your dog knew better." It is all on you.

RELIABILITY

Your clients are counting on you! Short of actual disaster, nothing should prevent you from showing up and doing your job. Do not run late, do not bail because something hindered you, do not quit without notice. Period. Once your reliability comes into question, it is game over.

If your client books you to take their dog at noon, they expect their dog to go out at noon. Making their dog wait longer could result in "accidents" or damage in the house. If you commit to arriving at a specific time, be sure you can fit that job into your schedule and arrive on time. If you cannot arrive on time and complete the tasks you have agreed to complete reliably and on time, you need to either allow more time for each client or book fewer jobs.

Having said that, life sometimes does get in the way, even when we are well-organized. If you are running a few minutes late (but only a few minutes late), once in a blue moon, you probably do not need to freak out. Let your client know you are arriving at 12:10 and not 12:00. A text message should suffice. Then, don't let it happen again.

We all understand, or should understand, emergencies happen. But you being sick is not one of them. Most illnesses come on slowly enough that you should have time to call clients and let them know the situation and that you will not be available the next day. They may not be happy, but at least you have not left them or their dog hanging. While any cancellation is not ideal, at least you would not be leaving them completely without options and giving them notice allows them some time to find an alternative solution.

If you know of another dog walker who could fill in for you, try to arrange for them to do so and give your client the option to use your recommended substitute. This should be their decision. Do not just have your buddy show up in your place.

Inclement weather is no reason to not show up, either. Just dress appropriately. If your client cancels because of the weather, that is an entirely different scenario. If you have a cancellation policy, your time will be covered by this fee.

NOTE: the only time the weather should impact dog walking is if it endangers the dog in your care. No one expects, or wants, you to walk their dog in a blizzard or during a hurricane! Mid-day, peak-heat walks during the summer in hot climates should also be rescheduled or kept short.

GOING ABOVE AND BEYOND
An added bonus for your clients that comes from hiring you is that they now have an extra set of eyes in and around their home. Of course, this is not really part of your job, but it only takes a moment to do the right thing. See a leak in the kitchen? Let them know. Is there a package waiting at their door? Contact them to check if they'd like you to bring it in (they may not). Is the dog's water bowl empty? Refill it. Whether or not this is part of your service agreement, make these courtesies part of your routine.

You are your business and as such, your reputation is everything. When you are just starting out, this is a blank slate. Of course, some people may be reluctant to hire you because they have never heard of you, but at least it will not be because you have a bad reputation.

Building a following takes time. Protect your reputation.

SETTING PARAMETERS; CREATE THE BUSINESS YOU WANT

Before you walk your first client's dog, you should develop a clear view of the business you want. Locations, numbers, and hours of operations are all important to pre-set in your mind and in your business plan. Even limiting the types of behaviors you will or will not except, should be clear to you before you can articulate them to clients. Otherwise, you may quickly find yourself taking on far more than you can handle.

SETTING YOUR FEES

When first starting out you may not know how much to charge for your services. Look around and see what your competitors are charging. Then decide where you want to be relative to them.

Most dog walkers maximize their time, and per hour income, by walking several dogs at once. You could offer one-on-one services for dogs that do not do well in a pack or who have special needs, just be sure to charge appropriately. If you choose to offer exclusive services, such as longer walks, trips to a dog park, or basic training reinforcement, set those fees accordingly.

Decide if you want to compete on rates with your fellow dog walkers or if you want to be a higher-priced dog walker who may have fewer clients but who gets paid more from each one. Alternatively, you could go the discount price route and charge less but have many more clients to choose from.

With time and experience, you will almost certainly change your fees and fee structures. The more in demand you are, the higher your fees can and should be.

Chapter 7.

LOCATION

Decide on your self-imposed boundaries. How far will you be willing to travel for a single client? What if there are two dogs in the household to be walked, or two clients in the same vicinity who are willing to commit to a schedule that works particularly well for you? What distance is simply too far? Only you can decide how far is too far, but the economics should play a role.

Calculate your costs and the time it will take to get to a distant client's home or business, and then return home or go to the next client's home. Either accept those costs as an investment toward expanding your client base or adjust your fees or fee structure to make each trip worthwhile. Many clients will agree to pay a travel surcharge for the right dog walker.

When thinking about your geographical boundaries, start to plot your walking paths. Have a clear route (or several routes) for each area you agree to work in. For each new client, you should know which are the best, safest, and most enjoyable walking routes.

NUMBER OF DOGS

If this is the first time you have walked dogs professionally, start with small numbers. Start with one at a time. Professional dog walking is not as easy as it looks. Over time you will know what is the maximum number of dogs that you can efficiently, effectively, and safely walk at once.

Of course, dogs from the same household who are used to living together should be able to be walked together from day one. Even if at home they do not particularly get along, during a brisk, no-nonsense walk, they may.

Do not take on more dogs than you can handle just to make more money fast. Any short-term gains can be lost in a nanosecond if a dog gets out of your control and is subsequently hurt.

<u>HOURS OF OPERATION</u>
You get to decide on your availability.

Do you want to dog walk full-time or part-time? Will you work weekdays only? Will you work evenings? Holidays?

Do not put your clients' dogs -or yourself- in danger by walking in the dark or working so many hours you can't think straight. Set work days that work with your other commitments. You can always add an extra day or two here or there when you have downtime.

It will be tempting, especially at first, to agree to work crazy hours. That might work for a while but is not sustainable. Once you reach your max limit on the days and hours you have scheduled to work, stop booking. This might actually work to your advantage. By creating a waitlist you create the aura of a service in demand (which you obviously would be).

<u>WHICH DOGS?</u>
Decide which animals you're willing to take on.

- Perhaps you live in a large city where most people live in high-rises. You may only want to take on clients whose dogs are small enough for you to pick up (limiting "accidents") when riding in elevators. You could decide to only take on dogs that are housebroken so that you never walk into a mess.

- Alternatively, you could offer yourself up as the "puppy whisperer", for those little ones with small and underdeveloped bladders.

Chapter 7.

- You could create a business model around "problem" dogs, dogs that other dog walkers have given up on.

Other limitations might include:

- No females in season (or solo walks only for them)

- No mixing of large and small dogs (who would struggle to keep up)

- No dogs with serious underlying medical conditions (alternatively, this could be a market niche you could tap into)

This list is far from finite. And any limitations are completely your choice. Be sure that any self-imposed restrictions do not overly limit you and keep you from reaching your financial goals. Be open to changing those parameters.

<u>SETTING FEES</u>
There are many models you can choose from when setting your fees as a dog walker.

Most dog walkers determine how long each walk will be and charge a single flat rate per walk, per dog. But you could create a different matrix.

You could charge a flat hourly rate and each client could choose how long a walk they want to reserve for their dog. Or you could charge per the visit and vary the length of the walk depending on the weather or to suit the condition of the dog.

A good idea would be to offer a discount for multiple dogs from the same family. Another discount could be offered for clients prebooking a large number of sessions or who contract for daily walks.

Have a plan and fee chart for charging for the unexpected.

If an emergency arises (through no fault of yours), do you want to charge a fee for dealing with it? What if that emergency causes you to be late for another client; how would you want to be compensated? Ask other dog walkers what they do and how much they charge. Set a fee and if you find it does not work for you, change it later.

Charging too little might be a red flag to some potential clients. Alternatively, do not push the envelope too much and charge what the market will not bear. Look around and see what others charge; that is always a good place to start. And then adjust accordingly.

ESTABLISH EMERGENCY PROTOCOLS BEFORE YOU NEED THEM

Have plans to care for emergencies. How will you get a dog home or to the vet in an emergency? What would you do if you encounter an emergency at your client's home? While unlikely and hopefully never to happen, things do happen. Sometimes bad things happen. While you cannot plan for everything, you can plan for many. Ask other dog walkers what they have done or would do in these scenarios.

Have a plan to cover personal emergencies that would keep you from showing up. One effective and efficient way to ensure your clients are well taken care of, no matter what happens to you, is to team up with another dog walker. Find a fellow dog walker (you will soon meet them all!) with a similar style and work ethic. Ask to be each other's backup. That way if you or they get sick, you can cover for each other. Be sure that you each let the others' clients know of this relationship long before it is needed. You must get the approval for this arrangement from each client. Make this part of your contract.

Remember, your backup will not only have the keys and access to your clients' homes, but they will also be responsible for "your" dogs in your name, so choose your backups wisely.

Alternatively, if you set up your business with a partner, you will have a built-in backup for all your clients. Building a business with a trusted partner can not only be a lifesaver, but it can also lighten the load and can even be fun.

NOTE: When writing your standard agreement for your clients, do not forget to address as many of the 'what ifs' as possible and clearly spell out what your solutions are.

DOG WALKING IS NOT A STROLL IN THE PARK; IT'S YOUR JOB

Professional dog walkers work hard. You will be on your feet all day. You may have dogs pulling at the lead for hours each day. Shoulder injuries are rampant in this field. There may be days you might miss a meal or two because a single dog puts you behind schedule. Be prepared.

But being prepared isn't just physical. It means showing up with the right tools, equipment, and attitude.

INVEST IN YOU.

Heading out with a good breakfast under your belt is not a luxury, it is a necessity. Being in good health overall is, too. Investing in your own health will pay off on the really hard days.

Invest in your mental health as well. It's amazing how much emotion and attitude runs right down the leash from you to the dog you are walking.

- Get enough sleep.
- Do your best to leave stress behind.
- Don't let one dog (or human) ruin the rest of your day

DRESS FOR WORK.

You want to look professional, yet you want to dress for the job. Since caring for dogs can be messy, no one expects you to show up in a suit or your Sunday best. You should, however, dress like the professional you are.

When you can afford to, invest in a couple of weather-appropriate shirts with your logo on them. Until then, choose clothes that say to the world you are a professional and you are ready to work: no rips, no stains, no smell. Avoid T-shirts with questionable verbiage or political statements even if you have strong political views. There's no need to compromise those views, but as a business owner you don't want to offend potential or current clients unnecessarily. You always want to project professionalism.

Do not overlook your shoes. Not only should they be comfortable (you will be on your feet all day) they should be in good repair (no holes) and clean. No one is suggesting you wash your tennis shoes daily, just occasionally or as needed. If you opt to wear walking shoes or hiking boots, keep them polished or cleaned with appropriate soaps.

NOTE: A word to the wise: break in all your shoes, particularly boots, before you schedule an entire day of dog walking. Your feet will thank you for it.

Finally, dress not only for success, but also for the weather. If you arrive at your client's home in shorts and a T-shirt when it is obviously going to storm, they may question your judgment. Even if you are one of those people who "never get cold" in winter, wear long pants, closed shoes, and a jacket; just choose as light a jacket as possible. For rainy days, you will not be able to manage an umbrella with multiple dogs on leads, so be sure to wear proper rainwear. When in doubt, pack for the worst-case scenario.

This all might sound patronizing, but it is remarkable how many dogwalkers find themselves out with a pack of dogs and caught unprepared in the rain. If there is any chance of rain, keep a slicker in your backpack. An added value of wearing a rain slicker, anorak, fleece vest, or winter coat is that you will have additional pockets!

In the summer, be sure to keep an extra shirt in your backpack (and replace it as soon as you use it). No one wants to see you show up at their door in a shirt dripping with sweat.

What else projects professionalism? Arriving with all the tools and equipment you may need.

INVEST IN A FEW QUALITY LEADS.
Some of your clients may provide you with a quality lead and collar, but not all will. Some may have chosen to buy an adorable, but ineffective, collar or harness for their dog. You should not use ineffective leads or collars, no matter how cute they are. Instead, bring and use your own top-quality equipment.

Make sure you have the right weight and strength lead for each dog. Do not use a lead intended for a Great Dane or German Shepherd for a Pomeranian. Do not try to make do with an ill-fitting collar, either.

Some professional dog walkers mandate their clients buy certain leads and collars or the dog walker provides them, at a cost, to their clients. Just be sure the dogs in your care are secured with the proper equipment.

Do not overlook the importance of the length of each lead; they need to be not too short and not too long. Long enough to give each dog room to maneuver comfortably, but no more.

If you walk more than one dog at a time you will need to take that into consideration when scheduling and as well as preparing equipment. If all your dogs are approximately the same size with the same stride, they all might do well with leads of equal lengths. If you mix dogs of different sizes, you will need to adjust the leads to make sure the pack moves together.

INVEST IN COUPLERS.
Couplers allow for multiple dogs to secure to a single lead. This will allow you to walk multiple dogs without your hands over-flowing with leashes. Most of your clients will not own couplers, so you will need to bring your own. Be sure that dogs attached by couplers are of a comparable size, walk at a similar pace, get along, and walk well together.

STOCK UP ON SUPERIOR QUALITY "POOP BAGS."
To say that you will need a lot of poop bags is an understatement. You will need loads of them! Buy the good ones. The cheaper ones are thinner and more likely to rip and who needs that? You could require your clients to provide them, although keeping track of "who used what" might be more trouble than it's worth. It is better to factor the cost of poop bags into your fee and provide your own.

KEEP A FEW OLD TOWELS HANDY.
No need to buy towels; ask friends for their old ones. These can be cut into smaller squares and can be used to clean dogs' paws, your hands, and whenever you need a clean wipe. Carry a few in your backpack. At the end of the walk, as you return each dog, wipe down their paws. It only takes a moment and your clients will appreciate it.

INVEST IN A TOP QUALITY, COMFORTABLE BACKPACK.
You want your hands free to manage the dogs but you will be carrying many items: Keys, phone, towels, water bottles, snacks, etc., etc. Put them all in a backpack. This is

a long-term investment. By buying top quality and keeping it in good repair, you may not need to replace it for years.

<u>YOUR PHONE IS YOUR LIFELINE.</u>
Just as you would invest in top-quality office equipment (if you had an office), you need to invest in your mobile office: your phone. Invest in the best quality phone you can afford. You may not need all the new "bells and whistles" but you might want the largest screen (for ease of use), one with a decent quality camera (for documenting your work) and one with great speakers (you'll be speaking and trying to listen over the sound of barking dogs). A single ear bud might work to overcome barking, but don't use both. You need to listen to traffic as well as your dogs.

You will want a phone and a phone/data service that is reliable and that can manage all the mobile apps you will need to run your business.

Be sure your phone is charged at all times. You do not want to find yourself in an emergency situation without phone service. If your phone will not hold a charge for an entire workday, you should schedule time to recharge it. Many restaurants are set up to allow you to charge your phone while you eat. If you do not plan to stop in a restaurant to eat, perhaps stop for coffee and charge it there. If that's not an option, invest in an emergency recharger and be sure that the recharger is full before you leave home.

Do not recharge your phone in a client's home! You should not be in their home that long anyway.

Preprogram emergency contacts into your phone. In case of an emergency, even 911 might be too much to remember (it happens). Program it in, just in case. Additionally, add a few local numbers to your in-phone address book such as veterinary clinics in your immediate area, fellow dog walkers, your local dog rescues, and animal control. Have them clearly marked and easily accessible.

Your phone is crucial and always having it charged essential, but stay off it. While you have dogs in your care you should be focused on them. Do not surf social media while you are working. Do not chat with your friends. Do not shop online. Should you answer if you get a call from a client? Maybe, but keep it short. Consider setting up your voicemail with a short message explaining that you are out with dogs and cannot speak but will call them back as soon as you can.

A good trick for handling incoming calls from clients is to assign a distinct ring tone to clients. That way, even without looking, you'll know whether or not to even consider answer those calls. While you are out with dogs, avoid texting, even for those clients who prefer it. Your hands are full enough with dog leashes.

Of course, if a client whose dogs you are currently walking call you, take those calls as they could be time critical.

If at all possible, use ear buds so your phone can stay out of your hands.

Yes, sometimes it's a little lonely and even a little boring walking some dogs; that doesn't matter. Stay off your phone and focus on your responsibilities.

One last word about your phone: protect it. Do not carry it in your back pocket to prevent it accidentally falling into a toilet. Stow it in a safe place when it is not actually being used to prevent accidentally leaving it in a client's home. Keep it away from the dogs.

Now that you are properly equipped, let's get walking!

Chapter 7.

WALKING THE DOGS

Finally! You are heading out for the day, completely equipped and ready to work. Great! What do you do?

PICK UP

Whether your client is at home when you arrive, or you are letting yourself in, be sure to secure the dog immediately. Don't just swing the door open; open it slowly and proceed carefully. Open the door only as much as you need to enter and close it quickly behind you. Some dogs will charge the door, others will try to hide from you. The ones of most concern are those who will try to escape through the opened door. Be prepared to block the dog from escaping. Once you have a relationship with each client's dog, you will know what to expect.

As you enter your client's home, validate your arrival. If your client is not home, you could text them letting them know you have arrived. If entry to the home was done using a smart entry, your clients may receive a message letting them know you have entered their home. This step will help minimize or eliminate any dispute about how long you spent with their dog.

Immediately secure the dog on the leash provided or the one you have brought with you. Have the dog completely under your control before opening the door to begin their walk. Check and double check that you have the key to this house *before* you exit. Then lock the door behind you.

If you are walking one dog at a time, simply take each dog for the length of walk you have committed to. If you are charging for a 30-minute walk, then the walk should be no shorter than 30 minutes. If the client contracted for a 45-minute walk, be sure that walk is no shorter than 45 minutes (unless extreme weather prevents that). The time to establish how long a walk is when you are hired. If, after working with that dog once or twice, you conclude the length of time is too little or too much, let your client know this. This is particularly true for puppies. Puppies need to be walked frequently but for shorter times. Longer walks will not help in potty training and typically very young puppies cannot walk for long anyway.

<u>THE WALK ITSELF</u>

Once you have your clients' dogs in hand, what do you do? How do you safely and professionally manage the walk?

- Take the route that you have already chosen as one that suits each dog and is safe.

- Check the leash and clasp occasionally.

- Walk at a pace as briskly as the dog, or pack, can manage.

Most dog owners want their dog to not only potty on their outings with you, but to get a bit of exercise as well. Do not force the dog to walk faster than it is able to, but keep up a good pace. You will need to use good judgement as to how fast to walk and when to stop. Once the dog has relieved itself, you can usually pick up the pace and not stop to sniff every light post.

There is one caveat to this: there are dogs that will defecate several times before they are "done." Pay attention to why the dog wants to stop and allow them the time they need.

Even if they've completed "their business," do stop occasionally. Remember, this walk is for them, not you. Let them stop and "smell the roses", or fire hydrants, from time to time.

Always consider the age and health of the dogs you walk. Adjust length and pace of walks to suit them, not you. If you are walking multiple dogs at once, make sure the pack is homogenous; don't try to walk older or obese dogs with young, healthy, fit dogs. It is not fair and can end badly. Walk older dogs together or singly. Help your overweight clients reach their target weights and fitness levels before introducing them into a pack that otherwise would strain them.

Clean up after the dogs in your care immediately and completely. No one wants to step in dog poop. Be a good citizen as well as the professional you are by cleaning up thoroughly after each dog. Then dispose of the waste properly. Each locale has different rules, laws, and expectations for what to do with dog waste. Learn what needs to be done in your area and do it.

As you walk, watch for, and anticipate, dangers. These include broken glass or other foreign objects the dog might try to eat; cars pulling in or out of driveways; aggressive dogs crossing your path; stray animals. If you suspect a wild animal in your vicinity might be rabid, report it. If you suspect an aggressive wild animal is protecting their young, report it. If you see a stray dog or cat, contact the authorities or local rescues. All these may not be your responsibility as a dog walker, but they should be the responsibility of every citizen.

Be alert, protective, and proactive. The safety and the health of the dogs in your care come first.

WHAT ABOUT DOG PARKS?
It may be tempting to take your client's dog to a dog park; do not. Besides the fact that you are being paid to walk the dog, letting the dog off the lead means you have lost control of that dog. It is risky and potentially dangerous. Dog parks can be great, but they can also be a source of illness or parasites, as well as dog fights and spontaneous attacks. And of course, by letting your client's dog off lead, you run the real risk of the dog escaping the bounds of the dog park and getting lost or injured.

RETURNING YOUR CLIENTS' DOG HOME

When you and your client's dog return to its home it is not enough to simply shove the dog inside and leave.

You should let yourselves in and securely close the door behind you. If the dog's paws are wet or dirty, take a moment and clean them off. Then make sure the dog's water dish is full. If you have agreed to feed the dog as part of your service, now is the time to do that. Follow the feeding instructions given to you by the owner. Make sure you return the unused dog food to a place where the dog cannot get into it. Complete any other tasks you have agreed to do such as feeding a cat or fish, watering plants, etc. Once those are complete and the dog is secure as per the owners' instructions, now would be a suitable time to "check out" with your clients. Send them a text message letting them know you have completed your appointment for the day. Consider sending them a photo.

Now, with key in hand, leave, locking the door securely behind you.

Repeat for all subsequent dogs.

PICK-UP AND DROP-OFF WHEN WALKING MULTIPLE DOGS AT ONCE

When you get to the point that you are walking dogs from different households at the same time, you must, absolutely *must*, plan your entrance and exit into homes with that pack of dogs. This is not easy and may in fact may not be possible unless most of your clients are at home and can hand you their dog at the door.

When a client meets you at the door to hand you their dog, pay particular attention to the lead, collar, coupler, and all clasps for each dog to make sure they are in good repair *before* heading out. By mandating your clients only use equipment you approve of, faulty equipment can be avoided. Always have a few extras on hand. You do not

106

want to be running after a dog on the loose with a pack of dogs!

If you have dogs from other households with you, you must have a way to secure them while this exchange is taking place. The same will be true for drop-offs at the end of walks.

One option is to tether them around your waist or to your belt. There are also cross-body leashes that can be used as your tether points. These cross-body leads are not recommended for use while walking multiple dogs (you will have little control over a pack that way), but for the few minutes at drop-off, while stationery, this is a good solution for you.

BRINGING YOUR OWN DOG ALONG
Do you plan on your personal dog accompanying you on these walks?

- Be sure your dog has the personality, temperament, and discipline to do this. He or she also must be physically able to be on the go all day.

- Be 100% sure your dog is well behaved enough to enter clients' homes without causing damage or being a distraction while you attend to your clients' dogs.

- Be sure you, not your dog, is the leader of the pack while you are walking.

- If you take on a client whose dog simply cannot be walked with your dog, you must either leave your dog at home that day or turn down that job.

ADDITIONAL REVENUE STREAMS
Because dog walking is so physical, you may not have the energy for adding more revenue streams to your business. But if you do, here are a few that might work well for you.

PET SIT
There is no reason you cannot pet sit and still keep up with your dog walking clients. You could choose to sit for animals that do not require walking and only need limited attention such as fish, birds, or cats.

WRITE
Of course, you would not be required to write about pets or animals, but what a great opportunity to do so! You could write about the pets you care for, or your adventures along the way.

ONLINE RETAIL
Managing an online store is something you can do at the end of the day or on your days off. Focus on products you use in your dog walking business, at least initially.

Since this type of business is significantly different from dog walking, with different legal requirements, you should consult with a CPA regarding your tax collection and payment requirements. You may need a separate business entity for this.

BITS AND PIECES FOR DOG WALKERS
- Be professional. In some ways you are competing with the kid next door. Offer added value.

- Earn trust and work to keep it.

- If it becomes necessary to end a contract, or fire a client, do not just quit, or fire a client without notice. You need to do your utmost –absolute utmost– to give notice. The exception to this of course would be a situation where you are not safe. In that case, you take care of you first.

- Know your limits. Do not take on more than you can safely handle on any single walk. With time

Chapter 7.

and experience you will be able to maximize your income for a given block of time.

Chapter 8.
ANIMAL TRAINER: CAREER AND BUSINESS

Flexibility: Moderate

Investment level: Low to very high

Startup costs: $0 to hundreds of thousands of dollars for a facility (and everything in between)

Mandatory education: No formal degree or certification is required

Recommended education: Pet CPR, basic pet first aid, basic bookkeeping. If you are willing to invest in a degree, one in animal behavior can be useful; but experience (under a mentor), certification from a reputable institute or organization, continuing education (master classes) from more experienced trainers are expected

Necessary equipment: None

Recommended equipment: A few superior quality leads for dogs, suitable harnesses and leads for other animals, a few good-quality toys and lures, treat bag, clicker (for those employing clicker training), tablet, smartphone, suitable software, equipment and supplies unique to various types of training (obstacles, jumps, blinds, sleeve, etc.)

Legal requirements: Some jurisdictions require that you register as a business and set up accounts for paying taxes and insurance. If you intend to work internationally, you will need a passport and be sure to check local work permit requirements and tax obligations before you travel for work.

WHY DO PEOPLE HIRE PET TRAINERS?

Pet trainers are hired to instill better, or at least acceptable, behavior in domestic pets, primarily dogs and cats. There are also opportunities to train other animals, both domesticated and exotic. Even though many different species are trainable, this chapter will focus on domestic pets, particularly dogs, for a pet training business model. Almost all the suggestions and recommendations within can be applied to other pets and other animals that can be trained for homelife or work.

For a myriad of reasons, pet owners can find themselves needing help to get their pets to behave well. It could be that this is their first dog and they have no experience in training any pet. It could be that a particular dog has proven to be more difficult than any they have had before. It could also be that these people have taken on an animal whose previously learned behaviors are proving beyond their ability to correct, or they are worried they will do more harm than good.

It is a wise animal trainer who does not judge what came before, but who can focus on the animal before them and appreciate the opportunity to improve the situation.

It is also the wise trainer who recognizes that he or she is often training the humans at least as much as they are training the animal.

Since basic obedience training is about getting the pet to do what they already know how to do, the only challenge is connecting those acts with words or hand signals we humans decide to use as cues. Once the cue-response connection is instilled in their brain, a well-trained animal will respond to those cues (commands) every time.

Training humans how to properly give those commands is often much harder to do. Your people skills will matter.

Every dog already knows how to sit, no need to teach the act of sitting. But getting a dog to sit on command takes training. Getting that dog to sit when asked, without a fuss, without having to repeat the command, and 100% of the time, that is *good* training. The same goes for practically everything asked of our house pets, be it lie down, speak, or simply to walk nicely on a leash.

Animals that work in entertainment or service are trained in all the basic commands and then much more. Dogs do not typically climb ladders; dogs that work in the entertainment industry might. Pets are usually forbidden to open a refrigerator; knowing how and when to open a refrigerator door might be required of a service animal. Advanced, specialized training is also needed for security work or farm chores.

Animals fulfilling any of these roles need training and that's where a professional trainer comes into the picture.

HOW DO YOU BECOME A PROFESSIONAL ANIMAL TRAINER?
In theory, anyone can call themselves a pet trainer. They can even tack on the word "professional" and start taking on clients. But if you want to be a legitimate, skilled, professional trainer, you need to put in the time and effort to acquire the knowledge and experience your clients will rely on to achieve the well-trained pet they need and want.

TRAINER CERTIFICATION COURSES
One option to becoming a professional trainer is to study at certified schools. There are some great trainer-certification organizations and institutes. Unfortunately, there are also fraudulent facilities and teachers. There are no formal industry-wide oversight bodies governing or

monitoring these schools or institutes, so you will need to do your homework and choose wisely.

Virtual, online instruction is probably not your best option when it comes to learning how to be an animal trainer. There is a place for these online lessons but it's the interaction with an expert trainer, and the other students, that will get you the most knowledge and experience.

The thoroughness of any course you enroll in is very important, too. A course of just a few weeks, even if it is in-person, will probably not provide you with all the tools you will need to succeed as a trainer. Look for a rigorous course that is long enough and in-depth enough to allow students to learn, ask questions, practice, and review.

Insist on learning from instructors who not only know what they are doing, but who can relay that information to you, the student. Not all who do, can teach. Find good instructors.

Try to get recommendations from people you trust who have actually taken any course you are considering.

While you study you will probably be training, or practicing teaching techniques, with your own pet. For additional practice, ask friends to join you as students with their pets in mock classes. But, even beyond that home-based practice, you need to find opportunities to work with a wide variety of pets with all their individual quirks and personalities, and a wide variety of humans with all *their* individual quirks and personalities. Unless you have a wide network of friends with pets willing to attend your practice classes (even if you offer them at no charge), it is possible that the only practical way you will have access to practice clients will be to work under an experienced trainer with their own client base. Think of this as an apprenticeship, and the trainer as your mentor.

Chapter 8.

<u>GET A MENTOR</u>
Some future trainers hire an expert trainer to learn from instead of attending formal classes. Many trainers-in-training attach themselves to a mentor in addition to formal academy study.

Schools and institutes will charge you to learn; mentors/master trainers may or may not. They may offer to teach you in exchange for free labor as their assistant or in helping around their training facility.

Whether you seek out a mentor to supplement a training course or as your primary teacher, they should not only show you how they teach and train, but should also allow you practical experience, to take the reins so to speak, and instruct. Often, the best lessons are learned from making mistakes. Having an experienced mentor looking over your shoulder and correcting your mistakes allows you more freedom to make those mistakes without lasting harm being done.

Find a great trainer-mentor and learn all you can from their years of experience, their successes, and their missteps.

BEFORE YOU COMMIT TO ANY COURSE OR MENTOR
Before enrolling in any course, or committing to any mentor, recognize that there are many different methods of training. And there are different training goals. Decide what method of training best suits you and think about what types of training you are interested in teaching. Then find the best instruction for you to learn under.

EX-MILITARY OR LAW ENFORCEMENT?
It is very common for trainers, particularly dog trainers, to get their start in the military or within a K9 police unit.

If you have that background, your knowledge of dogs and training is likely far more advanced than others entering this field But they may not easily translate into civilian needs. Be cognizant of the different expectations and goals civilians may have. The majority of your potential client base are looking to train their pets for non-working goals, that is, living at home with a family. Despite your background, consider learning through a course or via a mentor how to work with clients who are civilians and how to train dogs for civilian lives, that is, unless you want to train animals for those specialized, service needs.

If you are interested in training dogs for security-related jobs, you already know that there is a market for dogs trained for police units or military uses and those agencies will occasionally look to the private sector to fill their ranks. Additionally, well-trained personal protection dogs for private clients can fetch top-dollars.

PROFESSIONAL TRAINING BUSINESS OPPORTUNITIES
So how can you earn a living as an animal trainer? For the moment, let's focus on just the dog world of training.

TEACH BASIC OBEDIENCE
Basic obedience generally includes sitting, standing, lying down, recall (come), and walking on a lead; all on command. Slightly more advanced training might include going into a crate or to a bed or perch; walking off-lead; or cute tricks such as shaking hands, again, all on command.

This is generally where all new trainers begin; it is a great place to start your business. The body of knowledge and experience you need is relatively minimal (but not nothing). Your investment in a facility and equipment is minimal. And there is an endless reservoir of potential students.

A few leashes and a bag of treats are really all you will need; besides your expertise, of course. Training classes can be held almost anywhere (but should be in an enclosed facility or fenced yard for safety) so overhead can be kept to a minimum until you are ready to rent or own your own facility. Is your backyard fenced? Train there. Is there a dog park nearby that is also fenced? Teach there. Once your business is more established, look for a professionally fenced yard or facility to rent. Boarding kennels and doggy daycares are often willing to rent out their facilities during off-hours. Consider partnering with a boarding kennel or doggy daycare where they not only provide the space you need and allow you to set up and store your equipment, but also can provide you with a potential client list, saving you time and money for marketing.

As your business grows and you gain experience, expand the number of services you offer. Offer ever more types of training. Keep a small inventory of preferred leashes and sell them. Buy in bulk the training treats that work for you and sell them.

ADVANCED OBEDIENCE

Many owners want their pets to learn more than just the basics. This might include all of the previous commands but at a distance or with the use of hand signals (not just words) to control their dog. Cute tricks like "rolling over" or "playing dead" might be taught in a basic obedience class, but they are more often taught in an advanced obedience class. Advanced obedience training also prepares dog-handler teams for obedience competitions.

Stay ahead of your students by learning how to teach these more advanced commands. Then, offer this advanced training either as part of a series for your current clients or a free-standing course.

TRAINING FOR COMPETITIVE SPORTS

There is a long list of sports for dogs (and other animals) for which professional trainers are paid and paid well. Your business could focus on one or more of the following sports:

- Obedience trials
- Conformation showing (cats can do this, too)
- Agility
- Rally or Rally-O
- Flyball
- Tracking
- Field work
- IGP (IPO/BH/Schutzhund)
- Frisbee or Disc Dog
- Freestyle (Dancing)
- Dock diving
- Herding

To teach dog-human teams to compete in any sport, you must be well-versed in that sport. You must know what it entails and how competitions work. You will almost certainly be expected to be involved in that sport (or were active in the past). Many clients will expect you to have been successful in that sport with the ribbons and trophies to prove it.

Each sport has its own requirements. Here's what you will need to have and provide in your business to train for these sports.

OBEDIENCE COMPETITION

As is true for obedience training, there is a wide range of locations and facilities that work. Choose a public one, rent or barter for one, or build yourself one. To lessen your risk and liability, only work in locations that are either enclosed or fenced (Even dogs that have had previous obedience training can have make momentarily and possibly dangerous decisions not to obey).

The tools you need to train clients to compete in obedience trials are relatively few and relatively inexpensive. Dumbbells and hurdles made of PVC, along with small traffic cones, are all you need to get you started. You could

118

invest in more equipment such as blinds, as you move forward. Since one mandatory trial exercise requires the handler to "leave the room", if you are training outdoors, buy or create a barrier behind which handlers can hide; if you train indoors, choose a location that allows handlers to step outside and return easily.

CONFORMATION SHOWING

Conformation (dog showing) is a lot more specialized than many outsiders think.

Each breed has its own standard and its own stand position when presented to the judge. You will need to learn the different handling (showing) styles each breed requires including how to stand a dog for inspection, how to move a dog around a ring, the proper terminology, and the various instructions a judge may give a handler. This is so that you can, in turn, properly instruct your students.

Besides teaching others how to handle, there are also lucrative opportunities for you in conformation work. You may consider becoming a professional handler as a side income for your training business, or vise-versa.

As long as you have a training area as large as the largest conformation ring, you will have no additional expenses to expand this type of training business as there is no specialized equipment necessary.

AGILITY

As opposed to obedience training that needs little by way of equipment, to train agility dog/handler teams, you must own, or have access to, agility equipment. This equipment (obstacles) can be costly.

You also need enough space where the obstacles can be set up. Some Agility obstacles, such as tunnels, can be toted around town, and set up in small areas. Others are simply too big to transport. Realistically, you will not be able to move an A-frame from place to place. If you do not have a large enough property of your own, you will need to rent space at a facility that does.

When looking for a facility, consider partnering with a boarding kennel or doggy daycare where they not only provide the space you need and allow you to set up and store your equipment, but also can provide you with a potential client list, saving you time and money for marketing.

RALLY OR RALLY-O
The investment and requirements for training for Rally are similar to agility, but slightly less expensive since the obstacles are fewer and smaller.

You will also need less space to train for Rally, than Agility, but you will need a facility large enough for the course as well as for your students to wait and practice in.

FLYBALL
While less expensive to equip than Agility, training Flyball teams does require a facility large enough to set up at least two courses (for mock competitions) and room to practice. Your facility should preferably be indoors. You will also need Flyball Boxes, Thrusters, Launchers, and Jumps.

Once you have a course set up, you can expand your business by offering your facility to outside groups and clubs as a site for competitions, for a fee of course.

TRACKING
This is one of the least expensive training businesses to set up. All you need is a large field and objects such as old shoes or boots, well-worn sweaters or sweatshirts, or other items that have been handled a lot to hide or distribute in that large field.

The best fields are agricultural plots where the items can be placed and even hidden among plants while tracks, or paths (usually made by tractors) are easily identifiable by humans.

Investing in a few tracking-length leads is also recommended, even if you mandate your clients purchase their own, which you will.

FIELD WORK

Depending on the type of field work, your investment in building a business for training teams for field trials may be minimal or considerable.

Like tracking, fieldwork requires an appropriately large, open space to work. It also requires some small, inexpensive tools like whistles and a few pricier items such as reflective vests, long leads, lures, and dummies. Cap or starter guns are also needed. Purchasing blinds and decoys can start to add up.

Be sure to secure any and all permits and licenses needed to train for or run Field Trials. Even if the land belongs to you, you may need permits to shoot, even if you are using cap guns or blanks.

IGP (IPO/BH/SCHUTZHUND)

To train dogs to compete in IGP, you will need all the tools and conditions for training obedience and tracking, as well as the equipment for proper protection work including sleeves, blinds, walls, and A-frames. This is a moderate to hefty investment. These items can be costly.

You will also need access to two to three training areas. You will train (and possibly hold competition) for protection work. It takes a large, flat, grassy area for this work.

The obedience portion of the IGP training could take place here as well, or it can be a different area (indoor or outdoor, although outdoor is preferred as competitions are held outdoors).

121

The final training area is a field for teaching tracking. This is fundamentally different from the area needed for obedience or protection work (see Tracking above).

FRISBEE OR DISC DOG
The equipment (investment) needed is minimal. You will need a supply of discs (Frisbees™) which is not a huge investment. Be sure yours are in fact suitable for dogs (not the hard plastic ones) and that they are always in good repair.

Since this sport takes place outdoors, your students need to train outside and not in a training room. At a minimum, you will need a good-sized yard to practice in. This needs to be larger than a typical city backyard but you do not need acreage.

Once you have more advanced students, they may want to create routines set to music. As their teacher you may need to provide a sound system at class.

FREESTYLE (DANCING)
While some Freestyle competitions take place outdoors, they are usually held inside. Any large room, garage, or carport will suffice as a training facility. Besides providing a practice space, you will be expected to provide a sound system for your clients.

As with many other sports, if you do not own a large enough space, you will need to either rent one or come to an arrangement with one. See if you can find a kennel or other training facility to use theirs. Be open to partnering with the facility.

DOCK DIVING
To train for dock diving you will need to provide a long enough pool with a suitable dock. This is an expensive investment. If you cannot afford one or don't have the space to install one, you may be able to rent access to a

pool. But since the dimensions and requirements are so specific, chances are you would be renting this from someone already training dock diving.

There is some danger associated with dock diving. You should train under only the most experienced dock diving trainers and once you start training other people's dogs, you should do so with an abundance of caution and care.

HERDING
This business can be an expensive one to start. Not only will you need to provide a farm or fields to work in, but you will also need to provide the sheep (or ducks).

Maintaining a flock of any size is itself expensive and can be a full-time job. If you already own and work sheep, great! You are ahead of the game. If you do not, you will need to arrange (i.e., rent) a flock that is already "broken to", or used to, working with dogs.

Little additional equipment is needed.

SPECIALIZED ANIMAL TRAINING
While dogs may be the most familiar to the public, many animals work in the following fields and training them can be both fulfilling and lucrative.

TRAINING ASSISTANCE ANIMALS
Assistance animals include a wide range of species. The best-known ones are dogs for hard of seeing or hard of hearing people. But they are far from the only ones. Dogs or monkeys, for instance, are trained to assist para- and quadriplegic people due to their dexterity. Assistance animals can act as living alarms for people living with epilepsy or diabetes.

Assistance animals, while beloved, are not pets. They are highly trained working animals. Typically, their training takes place at a professional training facility where they, as well as their prospective human counterparts, are thoroughly vetted and trained to work as a team. These animals go through rigorous training, long before being introduced to their future handler/partner.

For you to become a trainer of assistance animals you will need extensive training by a recognized governing body. Any reputable organization will require you to have a background in obedience training and they will require you to spend months under their tutelage, learning how to train both the animals and the people needing the assistance.

The certification of an Assistance Animal should be backed up by the hard-earned recognition of an organization working on behalf of people with special needs. "Guide Dogs of America" is one. "Helping Hands Monkey Helpers" is another.

An alternative, but related, field of animal assistance training is to train therapy or emotional support animals. Therapy and emotional support animals, while serving a deserving public, are not the same as service animals. These are often pets who have been given a job due to their particular affinity for giving comfort, but they are not trained to perform specific tasks.

As a trainer of emotional support animals you would be expected to teach the dog-human team basic obedience so that the support animal will be a "good citizen" and not a disturbance. This will ensure they are welcome wherever they go. Some trainers go further and offer classes that expose the team to less typical and potentially stressful situations to prepare these animals for the lives they will lead. These could include riding on public transportation, shopping in a crowded mall, or visiting a school or hospital.

Therapy dogs are also pets who have an affinity towards humans and have the temperament to be calm and comforting in hospitals or hospice environments. Some go into schools to be a support for young students. They must be well-behaved and usually need to pass a test from some authority to earn their therapy dog certification before they are allowed to visit patients.

Be wary of groups professing to train or supply emotional support or therapy animals but who are little more than puppy mills. It is hard to scam someone with a dog said to be trained for a seeing- or hearing-impaired person. But people are easily scammed when it comes to emotional support animals. It has become such a problem that businesses are finding themselves having to question *all* assistance animals to weed out those who simply paid for a vest and a decal.

Do your homework to make sure you are training under, and representing, only reputable legitimate organizations.

Do not rush into creating your own business training service or support animals. The investment may not be large and the ROI may be attractive, but this is serious work and should be taken seriously as people's lives are often on the line. Be sure you are truly qualified for this work before jumping in.

To establish an assistance animal training business, besides your experience and any certification, you ideally will have a suitable facility for training. You will need to house and care for the animals during their training and you may possibly want to provide housing for the people during their early days of being matched and training with their service animal. At the very least, you will need a facility for training the teams before they step out into the world to train in real-world settings.

TRAINING ANIMALS FOR ENTERTAINMENT WORK
There is a niche field of animal training where your "student" will get all the recognition and only your co-

trainers will know your name: training animals for work in the entertainment industry.

Everyone knows Lassie, but do you know the name of his (yes, Lassie was a series of male dogs) trainer? (Answer: Rudd Weatherwax.)

Animals are used in TV productions, in film, and even on stage all the time. You might have noticed the same English Shepherds in a number of TV commercials in the early 2000s. The musical *Annie* has had live dogs playing Sandy every day for years, twice on Saturdays.

Whether it's a dog, a cat, a bird, or a rat, to work as "an actor" these animals must be well trained and reliable in obedience. Time is money and no producer wants to waste time on an ill-trained (a less-than-100%-obedient) animal on their set or stage.

Some of their work may entail stunts, such as climbing a ladder or walking over a pane of glass. Actor-animals may be asked to fearlessly jump from a boat repeatedly during filming, each time looking enthused and not bored. Stage animals must be able to hit their cues without being distracted by the collective "aww" from the audience that accompanies their stage entrance.

This is an incredibly difficult field to get started in, but not particularly expensive. The investment in starting such a training business is primarily an investment of your time.

Most animal actors are trained by their owners and these owners are already experienced trainers. Many newcomers to this field start as assistants to these experienced and well-connected trainers. Learn all you can from these established trainers and then work with your own animals. Have your "actors" ready to audition and to step up at a moment's notice.

Chapter 8.

MARKETING YOUR TRAINING BUSINESS

The good news is that you have a product that no one else has: YOU! Be proud of your education and experience. You do not have to brag about it, but don't hide it either. Put yourself out there and market yourself along with your business.

If you document all you do you will have plenty of content to use for marketing. Shoot videos and stills of your work, your classes, and your successful students. Do not be afraid to document and share your difficulties from time-to-time. Invest time or money in getting your marketing materials edited properly.

Be sure to get written releases from your clients to use photos of, and write stories about, their animals training with you in all your promotional materials.

COMMUNITY INVOLVEMENT

One really good way to promote your business, and keep your name front and center, is to participate in community events and offer your services to community organizations. In addition to typical opportunities such as renting booths are local events (especially if you can't afford those fees) offer to provide a free demonstration at these events using some of the animals you have trained. It costs you nothing and costs the organizers nothing either.

If there are 4-H groups near you, offer to help the young members with training their pets or offer your training facility for their use at little or no charge. This is something that costs you little out of pocket but can lead to future well-paid work. Let the press and relevant podcasts know of your community involvement.

Offer reduced rates to members of local breed clubs or offer to speak with them about specific training issues.

On "professionals day" at local schools, offer to give demonstrations and speak to the students about animal training as a profession.

ADDITIONAL SOURCES OF INCOME AS A PROFESSIONAL TRAINER

Novice trainers should focus on increasing their training, knowledge, and experience and on building their following and client base. But over time, you may have the time to maximize or increase your income with additional, related revenue streams.

MAXIMIZE YOUR FACILITY

If you own your own facility, rent it out when you are not using it. You could rent it out to kennel clubs, competition organizers, or even to other trainers (though it might make more sense to simply hire or partner with them).

This revenue stream could begin from the moment your facility is ready for use.

ONLINE INSTRUCTION

Online instructional classes (webinars) or video series for simple, basic commands have become very popular. There is a lot of competition in this area but if you have what it takes and the time to market yourself, this can be lucrative.

HIRE TRAINERS TO WORK FOR YOU

Once you have maxed out your day, hire others! They can be employees or subcontractors. Be sure to train them in your way of doing things; after all, they are representing you and your business. Be sure the quality of their work and instructions meet the high bar you have set for yourself.

TRAIN FUTURE TRAINERS

Down the road, when you have the experience and credibility, consider offering classes for new trainers wanting to enter the field or teach master classes for established trainers looking to expand their repertoire.

RETAIL SALES

Sales of training-related equipment is a compatible business and can bring in a nice income. The best products to sell to your students are those products you love and can whole-heartedly recommend. Try to develop a relationship with the manufacturer or distributor to get the best deals and pass along savings to your clients.

You will not be able to compete with the big box stores, so don't try. Your advantage is your expertise. Be sure you *are* an expert before you start recommending products.

The sale of training products that *you* have developed can move your business to a whole new level if those items are either revolutionary or are significant improvements over existing training products already in the market. See Chapter 13. CREATING AND SELLING PET PRODUCTS, for additional information.

CREATE CONTENT

Write books, a blog, or a newsletter about training. In a short time you will have many stories and experiences to share. You could write an instructional manual or a narrative about life as a trainer. Your blog could be about specific training issues or about pet care in general. A newsletter can be both informative and a way to promote products or services that others will pay you to write about and promote. All of the above could be in video form if you can film your work or have someone who will video for you.

BITS AND PIECES FOR PROFESSIONAL TRAINERS

- Walk before you run. Invest the time it takes to learn to be the trainer you hope and envision yourself to be.

- Remember that you are often training people and only guiding pets to behave in a certain way on command. Shore up your people skills.

- Be generous with your knowledge but don't give it all away for free! When people ask for advice for dealing with their pets, share a few minutes of your time; it costs you little and could result in a new client. But don't let friends or acquaintances take advantage by having you train their pet for free. After a few minutes of advice, invite them to join your class.

- Nothing prevents you from becoming a professional trainer in several areas. Obedience trainers teach agility; IGP trainers teach obedience; field trial professionals teach tracking. Mix and match what works for you to broaden your appeal and expand your business.

Chapter 9.
DEVELOPING A PET PHOTOGRAPHY BUSINESS

Flexibility: Moderate to high

Investment level: Mid-level to very high

Startup costs: From a few hundred dollars into the thousands

Mandatory education: None

Recommended education: Camera and photography technique classes, photo editing classes, bookkeeping

Necessary equipment: As good a digital camera as you can afford, several lenses and filters, tripod, equipment case, light set, computer, editing software, high resolution monitor

Recommended equipment: All of the above plus background screens for in-studio work, props

Legal requirements: Establish a legal entity, business license, tax account, insurance

WHY DO PEOPLE HIRE PROFESSIONAL PET PHOTOGRAPHERS?

In an age when every phone is a camera and so many people continually document every aspect of their lives, including their pets', why would anyone hire a professional photographer? The key to this question is the word "professional". It is one thing to catch a pet being cute enough for social media, but it is entirely something else to capture the essence of a beloved pet at a quality level suitable for framing or for commercial use.

- Many people want their pet's photo hanging on the wall alongside, if not instead of, any two-legged children's portraits. Pets are also often included in family greeting card photographs; amateur photographers who are inexperienced at capturing animals may not be able to get that perfect photo for the Christmas card.

- Commercial use of pet photography obviously demands professional quality work and end products. Business owners, in and out of the pet industry, often use pets to market their products. Businesses, particularly those catering to the pet care market, may want photographs of animals to decorate their offices. It is a rare amateur who can take photographs sharp enough to enlarge to poster-size.

- There is a large market looking for top quality pet- and animal-related art.

- Pet photographers are hired to create images for publications. This could be for a magazine article or book.

- Professional breeders need top quality photos of their pets to be able to promote their litters and their pets' lineages. Owners and handlers of pet-competition winners always want a record of their successes.

- When people want to be *in* the photo with their pet, they are often open to paying an experienced photographer who will create the set or setting, take quality photos, and then edit those photos to produce the best representation for the client's business or home.

Chapter 9.

WHAT IT TAKES TO BECOME A SUCCESSFUL PET PHOTOGRAPHER

While it is possible to specialize, successful pet photographers are multi-disciplinarians, at least when they are starting out. As they increase their client base and, more importantly, their portfolio, many photographers will specialize in one or two sub-sectors of this market. All professional photographers would be wise to work toward becoming experts in as many areas as possible for both outdoor and indoor (studio) work.

Pet photographers doing outdoor work are like sports photographers on the sporting field; they take pictures of animals in motion as they work or play. These may be pets participating in sports or animals in the wild. The results are high-speed photographs which take much more than just setting your camera on a faster shutter speed. It requires understanding the animals being photographed, how they move, and where they are likely to be as the shutter clicks. It also requires understanding the sport or activity in which that animal is engaged to anticipate what comes next and where the "money shot" is likely to take place. It takes knowing how to be at the right place at the right time. It also requires patience to sit (or stand) for hours waiting for the right opportunity.

For in-studio work, pet photographers need a different type of patience.

During an in-studio or a prearranged outdoor photo shoot, the environment is more controlled and the subject is probably under better control than in the wild. But one is still photographing living creatures with minds of their own. Even the best trained dog can turn uncooperative just as the camera starts clicking. A dog, cat, or pet bird can decide it simply does not want to work and it will be game over for the day. Photographing exotic animals, even in a controlled environment like a studio, has unique risks and challenges.

The professional photographer needs to have the wherewithal to overcome these situations and complete the job.

Aside from the right temperament and the necessary photography and editing equipment, what do you need to bring to the table to be a successful professional pet photographer?

First and foremost, you need to be an excellent photographer in general. You need to hone your craft. It takes years and thousands of photographs to fully understand how light and angles affect a picture's outcome.

You need to know how to make the most of your equipment. Great photographers refine their "eye" and their aesthetics continuously. Try to get input from photographers whose work you admire. Plan to continue to take classes whenever you can.

Digital photography may have replaced the darkroom (though not completely), but good editing skills are still important and expected. Editing can not only make a good photograph great, it can sometimes rescue a shoot that has gone terribly wrong. Become proficient at digital editing.

Amass as much experience as you can, interacting with as many types of animals as you can. If you cannot find many opportunities to be in their vicinity before a shoot to learn first-hand about their behavior, read about them and speak with experts.

If you intend to limit yourself to working with dogs (or other domestic pets) only, that's fine, of course. But then you should invest the time interacting with them in as many different scenarios as you can. Learn their cues and warning signals. Learn how each breed moves and works so you can capture them at their best.

The more you know about the species you work with, the better your photography sessions will go, and the better your end products will be.

SPECIALIZED AREAS OF PROFESSIONAL PET PHOTOGRAPHY

As a new business owner just starting out, you will probably want to take on any photography job to pay the bills. That makes sense. Over time, you will learn where the market is strongest, where you earn the most, and perhaps most importantly, where you excel. Once your schedule is full (and you are earning a living wage), you will be able to begin to choose which jobs you take and start specializing in those areas and market yourself accordingly. Try not to narrow your scope too much or too early. You may be missing out on opportunities in the future.

There are many areas in which to specialize as a pet photographer.

PORTRAITS

Just as people will hire photographers to take family or individual portraits, so will pet owners pay to have their pets photographed. These sessions can take place in a studio, in the clients' homes, or outdoors.

For in-studio work you will obviously need a studio. The upside to this is your clients come to you. Your time is not spent traveling. Nor do you have to lug equipment around with you to remote locations. The downside to working exclusively in studio is that you have to maintain a studio. Unless you have space at your home, you will need to rent or buy a separate work space and this can be expensive.

On the bright side, your studio is a deductible business expense, even if it is in your home.

Keeping a studio clean can be a challenge when working with domestic pets. Inviting exotic animals to come to your studio can leave you with even more sanitation issues along with zoning and permitting restrictions. Before you commit to or invest in a studio, know what your local zoning allows and secure all the permits required.

Outdoor portrait work can be done in locations that do not cost you anything to use. Photographing wildlife in their natural habitat could cost you little more than the entrance fee to a park or reserve. Of course, it could cost you a plane ticket and hotel if you are looking to capture animals far from home. For domestic pets or local fauna, your local park or garden works great for many shoots of animals, with or without their humans.

Outdoor photography comes with its own set of challenges. Your equipment needs to be sturdy enough to move about repeatedly yet light enough to transport easily. Each session will require time for setting up and breaking down your sets. Being outdoors may leave you with no access to a power source. Investing in multiple back-up batteries, which can be expensive, is a must. Studio lights are not an option; lighting can be a challenge. There are distractions (which can be both a positive and a negative) and weather can prove a challenge and may result in cancellations.

Yet, natural light can create wonderful ambience. And being outdoors allows you to capture the pet in a more natural setting which can be more relaxing for your subject.

Become familiar with a few outdoor places near your home where you can easily bring your clients. Learn which locations make the best backgrounds and offer the best lighting.

Some photographers offer in-home photography sessions. But choosing to photograph pets in their home also comes with advantages and challenges. Your subjects may not feel as relaxed as you might hope, despite being in a familiar environment; your presence can itself be disturbing. The unfamiliar lights and cameras might feel threatening to some pets. That same equipment has to be transported, unpacked, set up, and then packed up for each session. And unless you are already familiar with your client's home, you will have to make split-second decisions regarding setting the room once you arrive.

But there are some advantages, too. Many pets will, in fact, feel more comfortable at home. There is no cleaning up for you to do after the session. There will be no special permits to secure. And there is no rent or mortgage to pay when using someone else's space. Travel needs to be accounted for, though.

Be sure to price your services based on the totality of the shoot. You should be compensated for your time setting up, breaking down, and traveling. In studio, buffer your prices to allow for cleanup and no-shows.

PET SHOWS
Some pet shows restrict photography to only those photographers hired by the show's organizers. You need to respect that, if you want to work in this sector. Candid photos of the show by any attendee are usually permitted and this can be a great way to build your portfolio; but check with the show's organizers before taking *any* photos. Check to see if those photos can be used legally for commercial purposes. If the answer is "no", just use them in your portfolio, not in your marketing materials.

Occasionally, individuals showing their pets are allowed to hire their own photographers to photograph their pets while at the show. Even if you have been hired by an individual, be sure you are legally permitted to do so by the organizers before signing any contract.

Besides taking pictures of animals being judged, there is a second category of pet show photography, that is the posed, staged photo op.

Winners typically get photographed with their handler and/or owner as well as the judge. The photographer for these winners' photos is usually hired by the show's organizers. If you are hired to work on behalf of a host organizer, be clear who owns the rights to those photographs.

Even those whose pets do not win, often want a photo of their pet with their handler, rider, or owner as a memento. If a pet owner has hired you to take posed photos of them and their pets, wait for the official photographer to finish and then ask for permission to use their backdrop for a few moments. Respect their response. Your good manners will go a long way in the long term. Besides, the response is usually "yes" anyway.

For all photography work besides shooting animals in their natural habitat, get a signed release from everyone you photograph. In this release, be clear who owns the rights to each and every photograph you take. Specify which photographs you can use for commercial purposes and what those purposes are.

When you are hired to photograph outside of your studio, be sure to calculate travel time, any admission fees, and downtime (time spent simply waiting between sessions). Set your fees appropriately.

Chapter 9.

PET SPORTS

As with human sport photography, pet sport photography is not for the faint of heart. It can entail being out in the elements for hours or days. You can shoot for hours and take thousands of photos before getting a few that are good and even fewer that are great. And that's only if you are lucky. Sports photography requires hundreds of frames to get "the money shot". You will need to be aware of a lot of things all at once: lighting, the action on the field, the other competitors, the crowd, and on and on. Even if you are photographing an indoor sport, this is hard work. You will be toting your equipment all day (unless you have an assistant) and on your feet non-stop. And you will need to protect your equipment more than yourself.

Capturing any athlete in motion is both a science and an art. If you want to be a credible and in-demand photographer at pet sporting events, put in the work to learn the sport, learn how the animals behave and move, and build up a portfolio. Knowing where the animal *will be* is very different from seeing where the athlete *is*. Learn the intricacies of the sport.

One way to learn is by attending sporting events and photographing for free (get permission first). The goal is not to sell any of these shots or even to use any of this work for commercial purposes. It is to learn and practice. And to make connections.

Another avenue for learning the intricacies of pet sports and how the participants move is to team up with trainers preparing these pet athletes. Practice taking photos of animals in action as they train. These trainers (and pet owners) may be open to this idea if you offer them free copies of pictures from these practice sessions that they can use in *their own* promotional materials.

What sort of pet sports are available for photographing? Dog sports (check the list in Chapter 8), horse shows, horse sports competitions, rodeos, county fair/4-H competitions, to name just a few. You could also go for the more remote sports like dog sledding or the more exotic like falconry.

You will need to invest in equipment suited for fast capture. Since things may happen quickly you will not have time to think about your next shot, you will just have to take it. Having an assistant to get your equipment ready for the next shot helps. If you can afford to, hire an assistant.

WHERE WILL YOUR REVENUES COME FROM?
Basically, if there are animals out "doing their thing," there is an opportunity to photograph them for a fee.

PET OWNERS
Pet owners love their pets and most want a visual collection of memories of them. They may take a lot of selfies or candid shots with camera phones, but these rarely compare with professional work. If the owner wants to be in the shot, they need someone else taking that shot. And if they are engaged in an activity with their pet, they'll also need someone other that themselves behind the camera. And that would be you.

FREELANCE WORK FOR INDUSTRY PUBLICATIONS
Magazines for pet enthusiasts will pay for photographs they want to run. If you are able to write a short article to accompany those photographs, the magazines will pay even more. Industry publications targeting professionals will, too. Get familiar with the many magazines and periodicals in the pet industry and see what they typically run. Submit your own quality work often.

Chapter 9.

Many pet related business owners use generic selfies for their promotional materials. As a professional photographer, you can do better. Build a niche creating great promotional art for pet industry businesses or for any business that wants an animal in their promotional work.

Over time, as your work and name becomes recognizable, this could lead to getting commissioned to work a shoot using an animal hired by the company. Or they may hire you with the expectation that you find the right animal for the professional shoot.

Companies may simply want to buy art from you directly from your existing portfolio. Be sure you own the rights to anything you are selling for commercial use. When possible, try to retain the rights to any art you sell from your portfolio so that you can reuse or resell it again; opt to collect royalties rather than sell photographs outright. If you cannot, you can still privately exhibit that work as part of your portfolio, you just won't ever be able to use it commercially again.

Another area of B2B clients are breeders or other industry professionals. Breeders need top-tier photographs of their top-tier lines for their promotional materials and website. They may be great at choosing the right breeding partners but may not be very good photographers. This is where you can step in.

HOW TO GET STARTED AS A PET PHOTOGRAPHER
It is all about your portfolio!

Before they hire you, people will want to see your work. Start your portfolio today. In the age of digital photography, the cost to take and store thousands of photographs at your disposal is less than pennies. So, get out there and shoot! Then organize your best shots in a way that not only shows your best work but tells a story about you and your work.

Once you start getting hired, do all you can to protect your brand. That means keeping your standards high and never letting shoddy work leave your control. Never, ever, share raw footage.

One way to ensure that your work remains top quality is to not overbook, which is tempting early on when you have bills to pay but little revenue. Do not solve a long-term problem with a short-term solution. It is better to work less at first and build a great reputation while honing your skill sets.

Creating quality art takes time. Allow enough time for pre-shoot interviews, setting up the shoot (or getting organized at events), post-production (editing), and post-production consultations (and perhaps reediting), as well as for the photography session itself.

PET PHOTOGRAPHY IS WELL-SUITED AS A PART-TIME PROFESSION.
If you cannot afford to do this full-time, start your pet photography business as a part-time side business. Many pet sports take place on weekends. Many pet parents only have time on weekends to have portraits taken. Once you are so in demand that you are getting overbooked, expand your hours. Still busy? Go full-time. Still busy? Hire an assistant for shoots and an editor for the post-production work.

MARKETING YOUR PET PHOTOGRAPHY BUSINESS
Photographers are in the envious position of having plenty of content for their own marketing material and social media. Use it to your advantage. Of course, it takes more than just posting an array of photos, no matter how great they are, to capture a following. But between your ready

supply of great, eye-catching art, if you can add a few well-chosen words, you have a winning recipe for social media success.

DO NOT OVERLOOK OTHER PIPELINES FOR ATTRACTING CLIENTS.

A good website is still needed. Your portfolio should be front and center, but do not forget to add good, current, relevant content as well. Update it regularly.

A beautiful business card with one of your best photographs is an inexpensive and quick way to spread the word about your services, too. Remember, you are an artist promoting art, so make sure your entire brand reflects that, even your business cards.

Be proactive in marketing yourself and your work. If you want your work to appear in professional and hobbyists' publications, contact and then really connect with their editorial staff. Reach out and introduce yourself and include a sample of your work (Be sure to watermark every submission until they are paid for). Pitch them your ideas for articles and photo opportunities.

The same goes for local news outlets. Print and online publications are always on the lookout for great photos that will attract their readers' eyes. Your local TV station may be interested in your work. It is a rare newscast that does not end with some feel-good story. An array of stills (or video if you do videography) of cute or attractive animals doing fun or interesting things is a great way for them to sign off. They will pay for freelance work. If your local newscast will not pay for your submissions, insist on being credited, or interviewed, as payment.

Do community work. Offer up a few of your photos for fundraising auctions. Loan an exhibition of your work to your local library or city community center. Offer to speak with civic groups or school classes about photography, particularly photographing pets. Offer to exhibit your photographs around town and in places where pet owners will see them. Loan businesses, particularly pet industry-related businesses, your photographs to fill their walls. Be sure to attach your business card to each photo with your contact information. The goal is to get your name, your work, and your brand out there and be seen!

If your goal is to collaborate with professional handlers or at sporting events, go to these events to get known. Go often. Speak with people (when they are not busy). Be nice. There is no need for a heavy-handed sell. Over time, you will start to be recognized and people will speak with you. Take photos and offer to send them to the pet's owner (or handler) on the spot, pro bono. If your work is good, they will recognize and appreciate it, and it can lead to paid work with no hard sell whatsoever.

RUNNING YOUR PHOTOGRAPHY BUSINESS
Besides attending to marketing and promoting you and your business, you will need to take care of the business side of things as explained in chapter 5.

In addition, you will need to invest in the proper tools of your trade.

PHOTOGRAPHY EQUIPMENT
Invest in the best photography equipment that best suits your intended type of work and of course equipment that you can afford. Wildlife or sports photography need lenses that in-studio work might not. Alternatively, in-studio work might need more filters and an array of backdrops that outdoor photography does not need.

While starting up a business usually involved investing money, there is no need to buy every single piece of equipment you might need down the road. Spend wisely and don't overspend.

Chapter 9.

Invest in the equipment you need. Take care of the equipment you have. Save up for the equipment you want or will want in the future.

<u>Darkroom equipment</u>
Your editing suite is as important as your cameras. Invest wisely and keep up to date with software. Do not be surprised that the cost for editing equipment far exceeds the investment you made in your camera and lenses. A well-equipped editing suite could have several screens, a top tier tablet and styluses, and a vast array of supporting software.

A tablet is useful for sharing your portfolio with prospective clients. The same is true for current clients reviewing the album you have prepared for them. Insist your clients review your work on a tablet, preferably yours, and not on their phone.

It should almost go without saying that you will need a reliable smartphone. Invest in a good one with a good camera. You will likely never use your phone as a replacement for a good camera, but it can be useful when you want to scout or test settings.

<u>Legalities</u>
One particularly important legal element that is unique to photographers is your photo release.

To protect your work, or to avoid receiving cease and desist orders, be sure to get signed photo releases from the owners, riders, trainers, or handlers of every pet you photograph. The last thing you want is to take a fantastic photo only to be prevented from using it.

While there are generic photo releases online for you to download, be very sure that they are sufficient and applicable to where you are working. Otherwise, pay an attorney to write one. It is preferable to consult with a lawyer and pay their fee once to get the best release you can, than have to go to court and possibly lose your rights to your work or your fees.

Create a unique watermark and use it! Your clients will usually want to see proofs to select from. When possible, do not let the proofs out of you control. If that is unavoidable, be sure to watermark each proof right across the photo to keep them under your control, up until the time you are paid and ready to deliver their final product.

Copyright all of your work.

INSURANCE

Be sure all your equipment is insured to the level of replacement. This includes your cameras, lenses, tripods, tote bags, backdrops, props, memory sticks, tablets, phones, editing suite, and printer. Choose an insurance agent who understands that your equipment is your lifeline and who understands the unique risks involved on your sets.

Get third party insurance to cover clients coming to your studio or meeting you at an off-site shoot. Do not rely on your client's insurance for any work done in their home or business; always have your own.

TIME MANAGEMENT

As was already briefly addressed earlier, schedule enough time for travel, set-up, proofing, organizing, and editing photos from each shoot. A shoot might last an hour, but pre- and post-production work might require many hours. The time spent on these activities should be factored into your booking fees.

You should also block time each day to attend to business correspondence, your business' financial health, and growing your business. It is quite common for photographers to hire an assistant (or a virtual assistant) who handles all their standard communications and bookings.

BITS AND PIECES FOR PET PHOTOGRAPHERS

- Art is in the eyes of the beholder. No matter how good you are or how sharp your photos are, you will not be able to please everyone. Try not to take criticism too personally.

- Use a rock-solid contract for all your clients. Be clear what you will provide, what will be deemed acceptable, and what will be deemed unacceptable work for which you will offer compensation. Make sure your contract protects your reputation as well as your income. As long as you deliver good quality work, refunds and discounts should be a last resort and should be at your discretion; that discretion should be made explicit in your contract.

- Have a rock-solid photo release form.

- Whenever possible, and it is almost always possible, get a non-refundable deposit for your work. People cancel for all sorts of reasons. Remember that this is a business, your time is precious, and once booked, you are turning away other jobs. You can always *choose* to offer a refund if you feel the reason for the cancellation is worthy of one.

Chapter 10.
TRANSPORTING PETS AS A BUSINESS

Flexibility: Low to high

Investment level: Very low to very high

Startup costs: Zero to hundreds of thousands of dollars

Mandatory education: From none to pilot's license

Recommended education: Basic pet care, animal CPR, bookkeeping

Necessary equipment: Depends entirely on the type of transportation and target market

Recommended equipment: Depends entirely on the type of transportation and target market

Legal requirements: Establishment of a business entity, tax accounts, insurance. Depending on the type of transportation and choice of business model, you may need: a license to operate, driver's license, commercial driver's license, pilot's license, passport, vehicle insurance

WHY DO PET OWNERS HIRE PET TRANSPORT SERVICES?
A pet owner might need a professional pet transporter for any number of reasons, relocation being the most common. Not all relocations allow for a pet to accompany its family while in transit, meaning the pet will need to travel separately.

Other reasons for needing pet transportation include:

- Delivering an animal that has been sold or adopted
- Breeding purposes

- Service or working animals may be rehomed at retirement

Besides the general concern these animals, some of these animals have a real financial worth and both breeder or handler and the new owner want to ensure that nothing happens to injure or traumatize these pets in any way.

And it's not just domestic pets that need professional transportation services. All of the above could refer to farm animals, exotic pets, or exotic (undomesticated) animals.

Working dogs may need to travel on their own to their job.

Breeders of livestock can find themselves needing help getting their animals to new owners. Not all farmers or ranchers have the time to transport their own animals.

Transportation can be necessary for rescues, too. If an animal in need is any distance from a rescue willing to take it in, or if the forever home is a distance from the rescue, these animals need transportation. A rescue animal, or one traveling for medical care, may need special permits or special accommodations. These special needs may require more knowledge or skills than the average person possesses.

And even in cases where a family pet is able and allowed to travel with its family or handler, transportation details are sometimes best left to an experienced professional. Transporting an animal across borders can be tricky; it definitely requires proper paperwork and planning. If a family's relocation happens quickly, they may not have the time to deal with all the bureaucracy and details.

Even without complications, some people prefer to leave any uncertainty or hassle to professionals. And that's good for you, as the owner of a pet transportation business.

Chapter 10.

WHAT DO YOU NEED TO BRING TO THE TABLE?
Logistics, be it for products or pets, requires tools, skills, and knowledge. It is more than just "packing and tracking."

The process to transport animals begins long before the day of departure. The transportation expert needs to know everything about the process. Flight times, regulations, and restrictions all fall under the heading of things you need to know. If your animal transport logistics company includes ground transportation, you will need to be familiar with roads and routes. You will need to stay up to date with tolls, construction, and weather issues.

It will be up to you to ensure that pet owners know what is legally required to transport their pet. You must be able to provide accurate and up-to-date information about immunizations and vet exams, travel conditions, and quarantines, just to name a few. Your clients expect you to know precisely what is required and that you will follow through to ensure all forms are filled out and handled properly and procedures followed.

Making your life a little simpler, state and federal agencies charged with overseeing both domestic animals and livestock provide this information on their websites. They also provide the required forms. International animal travel guidelines and procedures can be found through airlines or embassies for the respective countries. It will be up to you to be familiar with these agencies and how to access all this information.

While it may not be your responsibility to speak to their veterinary care providers or book appointments, you should be on top of things and remind your clients to get copies of all necessary veterinary forms and proof of exams and immunizations. You are responsible for informing them what, how, and when. You do not want to

151

have to deal with a stressed customer who has not complied and finds themselves with no time left to correct the situation. Not only will you be faced with an angry client (chances are good they will blame you) but you will lose the revenue as this transportation contract falls apart.

You also need to have a good understanding of basic animal care. The care needed to transport puppies is different from that provided for adult dogs; rescue animals may need different care and attention than those needed for family pets accompanying their families on the same plane. How much water; how large an enclosure; how often to stop to "potty"; to feed or not to feed; all this information needs to be in your wheelhouse.

You must be familiar with all the enclosures available and know which works best for a myriad of situations. The same is true for all the accessories needed for transporting animals.

If there are particularly popular destinations for your target market, collect as much information as you can about those destinations on behalf of your clients. Providing a list of recommended vets or pet food suppliers may not fall under the heading of transportation, but it's an easy added value service.

Other bits of information you will want to have at your fingertips are: what your customers can expect from their pets post-travel and helpful bits of information about acclimating a pet to new surroundings. Think about the things you would want to know if it were *your* pet getting transported. Provide that level of information, service, and care.

Be highly educated about each species you plan to transport or have access to experts for those animals. You could hire those experts or contract them for advice as needed.

Chapter 10.

The more you know, the more your clients will see you as a reliable resource bringing added value for which they will be happier to pay. And the more likely they will be to recommend you and your services to others.

Only take on animals for which you have the necessary education, training, and facilities to handle safely.

BESIDES LOGISTICS: POSSIBLE PET TRANSPORT BUSINESSES

Organizing the logistics for travel is not the only business model.

For instance, It is not unheard of for a rescue to transport a large number of dogs (or cats) at once to keep costs down. Rescues may (and do) contract for buses or vans outfitted with crates and air-conditioning. You could provide that. Some rescues need extra sets of hands to help the driver care for the travelers: you could offer a travel companion service, regardless of the mode of transportation. You could build a business specializing in transporting special needs animals (for which you could charge a premium).

Be open to exploring different transportation services you might offer but keep in mind, each model requires slightly different skill sets, number of employees, investment, and time commitments.

PROFESSIONAL PET TRANSPORTATION BY VEHICLE

In theory, all you need to transport pets is a car. To be a *professional* transporter, however, you will need more; your clients expect and deserve more.

You will need a suitable, well-maintained car or truck. Suitability depends on which animals, how many, and how far. If you will be transporting one cat or one dog at a time, your vehicle should be outfitted with a single, secure crate. If you intend to maximize each trip, taking several dogs at once, you will need a vehicle large enough to accommodate a number of secured crates or car harnesses. Installing a secondary gate at the back of your van can prevent any animal that accidentally escapes from their enclosure from escaping from your vehicle. You may want to purchase a ramp so that older dogs do not have to jump in or out of your van. Transporters have revamped vans, campers, buses, and semi-trucks depending on the scale of their business.

Besides enclosures, invest in a number of slip leads, water and food dishes, a few basic care items such as brushes, tick removers, and even a few muzzles. You will need these for any long distance travel when you have to feed and walk the dogs or cats in your care. If you are transporting birds or other pets that can remain in their enclosures for days, the risk of escape is less (but not zero). They will still need to be fed and watered.

Basically, if you plan to transport pets or other animals by vehicle, you will need to invest in the appropriate restraints and equipment to get each and every animal to their destination safely and in good health.

Regardless of which types of animals you will transport, sign up for the best roadside service. Anticipate the worst and have a plan.

Before each transport, download maps and print out lists of emergency veterinary services along your planned route. Do the same for an alternative route or two. This falls under the heading of anticipating the worst. You do not want to be lost, or in need of medical care, only to find that you are without internet connection.

Create an "employee manual" including procedures and protocols. Even if you are a one-person outfit, write these down. In an emergency you may not have time to think and your manual will clearly spell out what to do.

Chapter 10.

You may be surprised to learn there are airline companies whose sole business is transporting animals; no human passengers allowed. Other pet airlines allow owners or handlers to accompany the animal, but the airline is first and foremost pet-centric. Some will fly anywhere according to their customers' needs. Others have set routes where, much like airlines for humans, their passengers can only leave from designated airports and will only land at pre-set arrival airfields.

As you can imagine, starting such a company can be expensive. At least one plane has to be bought or leased and then maintained. These planes need to be outfitted with secure cages and supplies. Unless you yourself are a pilot, pilots and attendants need to be hired and salaries paid. The reservations office needs staffing. And everyone involved needs to be educated in basic animal care, pet CPR, and the laws and regulations governing the transportation of animals.

If that sounds like the kind of business you want, and you have the resources to invest, go for it. Others have. And some are still around and profitable.

An alternative to starting a business with an entire fleet of pet travel planes, is to start small.

If you are a pilot, you could, much like the previous van driver, transport an animal or two yourself. If you own a plane, you could outfit that plane with a crate or two and take on clients at will.

If you are not a pilot, do not own a plane, or choose not to do the flying, find a pilot who will. Pilots of small aircrafts are often looking for passengers who will simply pay for the gas allowing the pilot to do what they love, which is accrue flight time. You will find pilots at every airfield and hangar. Your fee structure will need to cover paying the

155

pilot's fee (if they ask for one), landing fees, plane rental, and gas. Compute a fee for your clients that covers all those expenses and don't forget to add your management fee and profit margin.

NOTE: If you choose to work with pilots ad hoc, you should know that the FAA (Federal Aviation Administration) has rules governing payments for "hiring" pilots who are not commercially licensed. Ultimately this responsibility falls to the pilot, but you would not want to be responsible for sanctions against anyone. Once you are familiar with the FAA rules and regulations and can work within them, you could amass a cadre of pilots willing to work for you.

A strict series of protocols and procedures need to be established that take into consideration this particular mode of transportation.

- Most flights will cross jurisdictions. Crossing jurisdictional borders means you must be in compliance with the rules and regulations at the point of departure as well as the destination.

- The care of the animals begins pre-flight and should continue to the point that they are safely enclosed at their new destination.

- Just as was recommended for vehicle transportation, create an employee's handbook, even if you are the only employee. Keep an indexed hardcopy with you at all times and refer to it as needed. Make sure your protocols are in alignment with the protocols pilots are obliged to fly under.

- Create a database of emergency veterinarians for each route you take before you (or your pilot) leave and print it out. Just as was true for ground transportation of animals, do not rely on using an app to find an emergency vet on the go. Apps crash. Wi-Fi and phone services fail. Plan for delays by having emergency supplies including water and possibly even pet food (as well as food for all the humans on board).

PROFESSIONAL PET TRAVEL COMPANION

If a pet is traveling alone, there are many points along the way where trouble may arise. Having a human companion to deal with these hurt points can make all the difference between disaster and a successful conclusion. Many clients will pay for this service.

One upside for such a service business is that there are few out of pocket costs to you and working as a companion for an animal in transit takes no special skills. It requires no investment, except maybe a passport. You can partner this business up with work as a pet sitter (if the itineraries match) or with any personal wanderlust.

While arranging all the logistics for the transportation of your client's pet may not fall on you, you should be familiar with all the details, including rules, regulations, protocols and special needs associated with each trip. You will be the point person on the ground should anything go wrong.

If the pet is small enough to travel in the cabin of a plane, but the owner is not available, you can be (or provide) that human travel companion who accompanies the pet-passenger in the cabin. If a pet must travel in the cargo hold in the underbelly of a plane, having a human on that flight ensuring the pet was loaded, providing care for that pet at any stop overs, and then being at the ready as soon as the animal is unloaded, can lessen the risk of accidents, missed connections, and even catastrophic loss.

One way to get a start in this field is to team up with existing animal transportation companies who may be interested in your services without having to actually hire you as an employee. Relocation companies may be open to offering their clients your services, at no cost to their company; they may even upcharge for it. Or you can offer your services to rescues. Then, once you have a name for yourself, you can parley this experience into your own full-service company where you hire the subcontracted travel companions.

There are several models for setting your fees for this business. You could charge per trip, per leg, per mile, or per hour. You may require your clients to pay for meals and hotels or you may roll those costs into the booking fee. It is completely up to you how you charge; just be sure that you are covering all of your expenses, are paying yourself a fair salary, and are leaving room for a profit.

WHAT ABOUT TRANSPORTING WILD OR EXOTIC ANIMALS?

Whether it's for zoos or rescues, wild or exotic animals need special attention before, during, and after transportation or relocation. Their care requires a specific set of skills and knowledge. It requires experience. And it requires expertise in the red tape and regulations regarding these animals.

Despite the challenges, or perhaps because of them, there is a market for servicing the legal transportation of wild or exotic animals. Sometimes, all that is required of such a transportation company is to fill out the paperwork and coordinate for the trucker or airline that has booked the physical relocation of the animals. Other clients may need a full-service transporter that can pick up a particular animal and drive it to its end destination. Still other times, the relocation is international and will require not only coordination of the transportation, likely both ground and air, but accurate compliance with laws regarding the importation of live animals.

If you are going to specialize in the transportation of wild or exotic animals, you need to invest the time to learn all the laws and regulations covering this. Your protocols will likely be governed by governmental rules and regulations. Create a handbook and a set of protocols that not only include these but that also cover your and your employees' responsibilities.

Your fee structure will depend on the animal, the distance, the staff involved, and more. As you set your fees, be sure to address every aspect that is an expense to you and set a profit margin that reflects the amount of work and responsibility each contract entails.

DELINEATING YOUR PET TRANSPORTATION BUSINESS
Even before you start the process of legally establishing your business, there are decisions to be made and questions you need to answer.

- Which modes of transport and which services will your company provide or arrange? These will determine practically every other decision you make, including the choice of business entity.

- Will you work locally, nationally, or internationally? Certain types of pet transporters lend themselves to one or more of these options. Knowing in advance what your limitations are, will direct you to which licenses and permits you need to secure and will direct the scope of your marketing and sales campaigns.

- Which animals will you work with? This will determine what type of facility (if any) you need, what supplies and equipment you need, and what types of transportation are available to you. If you are only comfortable with, or set up for, dogs and cats, do not take on snakes or birds. You can always expand your business to include different types of animals later. Be sure to restructure your business plan to accommodate any changes if you did not include them initially. Be very sure you acquire the knowledge and staff you need to work with additional species.

Once you know where and what your business will be, you can create a business entity which best protects you and your assets. It will also determine which, and how much, insurance your business requires.

When building your budget, be sure to include every single expense of running what could be a very complicated business. The price of aviation fuel is not the same as the gas we put in our cars. Hiring a crew to accompany a plane full of domestic pets is not the same as the crew needed to care for exotic animals.

PROCEDURES AND PROTOCOLS
For the umpteenth time: develop procedures and protocols for every single aspect of your pet transportation business. Include procedures for documenting every action and decision made during the time any animal is in your care. This is a high-risk business with a lot of moving parts (literally) and many opportunities for disappointment and even disaster. The better your protocols and procedures, the better prepared you will be and the better protected you and your company will be. Include issues such as loading and unloading; feeding; dispensing medications; and emergency procedures.

Share these protocols and procedures with your clients. Clients and potential clients will appreciate knowing how ready you are for anything that may happen.

Chapter 10.

MARKETING YOUR TRANSPORTATION COMPANY
The biggest hurdle in terms of marketing may be that people simply have no idea that animal transportation companies exist! As you market your own business, work towards improving the entire business sector by educating the public.

Consider teaming up with complementary companies or even with your competitors, especially those outside of your immediate area or those that cover animals or locations that you do not. Consider becoming a valued subcontractor for relocation companies.

Maintain a public presence on social media sites. Keep these up-to-date and relevant. Privacy may be an issue for some of your clients so respect that when sharing anecdotes. The same goes for sharing photos. But when you can get permission to share, do so. Try to get testimonials and reviews from satisfied clients that you can then share publicly.

Your marketing campaign plans need to address the various niche markets you are interested in serving. Create marketing campaigns designed for each market segment you want to work with. For instance, if you are interested in working with rescues long-term, your message to them may be slightly different from the message you send out to private families looking to use your service once in a lifetime. If military relocations are available to you, learn where you can best advertise your services on and near your local military base or post. Your core business doesn't change, and neither do your standards. But in wanting to meet your target markets where they are, the format, placement, or emphasis of your marketing materials may differ.

Many pet owners will turn to their vets to inquire about how to safely transport their pets. Provide local vet clinics with all your marketing materials.

You may want to try to partner with travel agencies, movers, and relocation organizations. Find those that provide the level of service you want to be associated with and see if they will not only promote your service but will also designate you as their "official" pet transporter of choice. Link their website to yours and vice-versa.

To offer your services to breeders, you first need to prove to them you are reliable. Find breeders where they gather and introduce yourself. You can find them online in breeders' groups or by contacting local and national breed clubs. Be present (take a booth or advertise) at pet shows and competitions. Advertise at or sponsor other animal-related events. Talk to them and listen to their concerns. Offer to give a short talk to their membership at an upcoming meeting.

If you want to focus your business on transporting livestock

- Contact farmers directly
- Advertise or sponsor agricultural events such as state fairs and 4-H events
- Build a relationship with large animal vets

Another target market you might want to focus on are professional animals. Included are animals traveling to work (animals working in the entertainment industry, for instance) or those that participate in sporting events and competition. For the most part, working and sporting animals will travel with their handlers, but not all do and not always. Even when they do, it can be a real service to those handlers to know the needs of their pets or team partners are being met because they consulted with or hired a professional to help take care of them. If the animal is traveling alone, your services could make all the difference in getting that very expensive working animal to their destination safely.

Clients coming from the professional animal care sector are different from private individuals, as they are likely to be repeat customers. Not only that, but they have connections with others in their field who might also become customers and, in turn, repeat customers. Marketing to them should focus on building longer-term relationships.

But of all the professional groups looking for pet transportation, pet rescues are probably the most prolific. They can keep you busy for sure. The challenge is, they are usually not flush with money and rely heavily on volunteer transporters. Do not despair, there is an opportunity here.

While you may not be able to sustain an entire business by transporting rescue animals, the good-will created by helping out rescues can often results in a great ROI from paying clients who appreciate your good works. The PR from doing good works cannot be overstated. Let your local news outlets know when you are about to leave (or return) from a trip on behalf of some local rescue. It is just the type of local, feel-good story that news directors love. It may help the rescue you are working with get some airtime, and it will reach a lot of people (free advertising) at no cost to you.

EXPANDING YOUR BUSINESS, ADDITIONAL REVENUE FLOWS
One way to expand your pet transportation business is by adding additional species to the list of animals you have chosen to work with. If you can transport dogs, you should be able to transport cats. If you specialize in birds, you

may be able to pivot to lizards and reptiles. Go slowly in this direction and be sure you have the necessary skills and knowledge needed to do this properly.

A second, organic, additional source of income could come from the retail sale of transportation supplies. This could be for individual clients or you could go "all in" and become a wholesaler of supplies for other pet transportation companies. You can set up an online store for this and either have purchases drop-shipped directly from the manufacturer or invest in inventory and ship out your products yourself.

Once your business is up and running smoothly, you may want to take on employees as a way to expand. If you have chosen to be a traveling pet companion, you can only be in one place at a time. But by hiring others to work for you, you could offer your clients a travel companion from an entire fleet of experienced travelers.

BITS AND PIECES FOR PROFESSIONAL PET TRANSPORTERS

- Get insurance and be bonded. Speak with insurance agents experienced in this area. Shop around for good deals but go with the insurer that offers the best coverage and the best servicing of claims.

- Keep all your relevant licenses up to date.

- Keep your mode of transportation in perfect working order.

- If you include international travel in your list of services, keep your passport up-to-date.

- Be clear, in writing, about what your services include, what they do not include, and how much you charge.

- Document! Clearly document every step along the way while your client's animal is in your care.

164

Chapter 10.

- Establish and follow well-thought out and articulated protocols and procedures.

- It only takes one catastrophe to collapse your business. Secure, secure, and secure again your clients' animals!

- Get as many emergency contacts as possible. Get backups to the backups.

- Have a credit card on file from each client just in case any of their pets in your care need medical care.

- Get a deposit and if possible, get paid in advance. At the very least, have a non-refundable cancellation charge and make sure that payment is made before you turn down other work.

Chapter 11.
GROOMING PROFESSIONAL

Flexibility: Moderate to high

Investment level: Moderate to high

Startup costs: Basic professional grooming equipment can cost as little as a few hundred dollars, while setting up a shop can cost tens, or even hundreds, of thousands of dollars.

Mandatory education: In the US there is no education requirement for working as a groomer, other countries may require certification from a formally recognized institution.

Recommended education: Grooming course, apprenticeship, pet CPR, on-going continuing education

Necessary equipment: Clippers and blades, scissors, nail cutters, Dremels (nail grinders), ear powder, blade oil, brushes, and combs

Recommended equipment: Depending on which model of grooming business you choose, you may need nothing but your own set of clippers, blades, and scissors. If you are planning to open your own salon you will need a tub, at least one grooming table for each groomer, stand dryers (at least one per table), crates or a crate bank, crate dryer, storage, towels, shampoos and other supplies, office space, basic office supplies, equipment, office management tools including relevant software.

Legal requirements: Some municipalities require that you secure a business license even if you work from home, pay taxes, and obtain insurance (even if you work as an independent contractor in someone else's shop). If you run your own shop or mobile van, you must have a business license and insurance. Mobile vans require DOT licensing and vehicle insurance, as well as business permits.

WHY DO WE NEED PET GROOMERS?

Groomers are the wonderful, almost magical, professionals who can take pets from shabby to chic. Dogs, which are the overwhelming majority of grooming clients, come in as hot messes and are returned cleaned, pressed, and folded.

But grooming is not only to make our pets look better; it is a necessary aspect of responsible pet ownership. It is important for the health and well-being of pets. A matted dog suffers terribly; so does a matted cat. Overgrown nails are not just noisy and annoying, they can lead to misshaped toes and are painful to walk on. A pet owner might overlook a tick; the professional groomer would not. And sometimes it is the groomer who is the first to find signs of medical problems needing veterinary care.

To meet those necessary and desirable needs, groomers offer a multitude of services from simple nail trims to full grooms (haircuts and styling), from pest removal to de-skunking the unlucky dog that took on a skunk.

As a groomer you can be a great resource for recommending pet supplies since you can speak firsthand about the quality of various products. You should strive to become a reliable source of pet care information.

WHAT DOES IT TAKE TO BE A PROFESSIONAL GROOMER?

Anyone can brush a dog. Anyone can trim their nails. Pet owners *should* know how to provide basic grooming care for all their pets. So, what differentiates someone who knows how to groom their own dog from a professional groomer? Experience, training, and depth and breadth of knowledge.

Professional groomers need to be able to properly groom a wide variety of dog breeds and complete each groom accurately time and time again. They are trained on how to get as close to the ideal cut as possible, even when the dog in front of them will never look like the breed standard. They can groom dogs of unknown ancestry and make them look adorable. Professional groomers need to be able to deal with a wide variety of dog personalities. They have been trained to groom difficult and even aggressive dogs.

Professional groomers, particularly those who own their own grooming shop, should be able to deal with a wide variety of human personalities, too.

The key to all this is proper training.

At the time of this writing, there are no laws mandating that groomers be certified or licensed in the United States. Many, if not most, grooming shops do not require their employees to have certificates from grooming academies. But all grooming shops expect their groomers to be able to do the job. Clients do, too.

NOT "AS SEEN ON TV"
If you've seen TV shows about groomers, you might have thought to yourself that it's easy. And through the magic of television, it certainly looks that way. But if you have ever tried to brush a matted or wiggly dog, you know it can be a challenge. Trimming nails, even if they are well-kept, can be a challenge. Removing ticks takes time and can be disgusting; so can bathing a dog that has rolled in a carcass or animal droppings. Now think about doing that repeatedly all day, five days a week. Add to that the challenge of working on scared, uncooperative, or simply ornery dogs and dealing with uncooperative or simply ornery human clients. It's not easy.

This is not to dissuade you from pursuing this career or this business. This should simply serve as a reminder and warning that grooming is not "as seen on TV".

Learning to groom, let alone learning to run a grooming business, takes time and effort. How and where can you get that training?

TRAINING AND EDUCATION
One way to learn to groom is through an apprenticeship.

Many future groomers start out as bathers. Bathing sounds simple but properly bathing a dog, or a cat, is a skill that needs to be learned. Learning to deal with dogs who are afraid or aggressive, takes time and guidance. Bathing a cat can be dangerous if not handled safely. If either is not bathed and rinsed properly (and basically remains dirty) the end result will be compromised and residual soap and grime can ruin the groomer's tools.

Over time, after proving themselves, the apprentice is trained to brush and prep dogs for the bath. They will be taught to trim nails (which can be a real challenge). Then they will be taught how to rough cut (taking off all the excess fur before the bath). Eventually the student-bather is shown how to groom easy cuts on easy (cooperative) dogs, graduating to ever more difficult cuts and ever more difficult dogs. In short order the novice has become an experienced groomer.

However, unless you are lucky enough to find a groomer who will train you, you will probably need to invest in a grooming course. Training courses run from just a few dozen hours of online instruction to months of daily classes and practical experience. It is probably obvious which one is the better option. By the time you have graduated from an extensive, respectable, reputable course, you will have been trained to groom dogs of a wide variety of breeds and from all walks of life. This investment may

170

seem steep at the time, but the ROI (return on investment) can be huge. Good groomers and well-run grooming shops can be very lucrative businesses.

Even in bad economic times, people will continue to have their dogs groomed. They may need to cut back on the frequency, but eventually they will realize that they cannot groom (or even bathe) as well as a professional and they will return to their groomer.

It is the wise groomer who continues to invest in training at professional conferences and by enrolling in master classes throughout their career. Factor continuing education into your budget and your schedule.

In addition to investing in proper training, there are personal tools that every groomer must have. And if you want to open your own shop, there are even more tools and equipment to invest in.

Make no mistake about it, grooming is hard, physical work. Professional grooming requires skill and stamina. It also requires start-up resources.

PERSONAL TOOLS
Just as professional chefs are expected to invest in their own set of knives, groomers are expected to purchase their own set of clippers, scissors, brushes, and combs.

CLIPPERS AND BLADES
There are many different clippers to choose from; you will want the ones that feel best in your hand and work best for you. For your clippers, you will also need to purchase a full set of blades. Actually, you will probably need to purchase a few sets of blades so that you can switch them out when they get hot in the middle of a groom or when they become too dull to safely work with. Clippers are not cheap and neither are blades, so do your homework and try out as many as you can *before* investing in the best quality

clipper/blade sets you can afford. There is no point in buying cheap tools if they wear out or constantly break down.

Whether you work for yourself or as a subcontractor in someone else's grooming shop, you will be expected to maintain your own blades. Find a local blade sharpener on whom you can rely. Professional blade sharpeners will almost always be able to sharpen your scissors, as well as blades, and usually can do minor repairs for clippers.

SCISSORS AND NAIL CLIPPERS

You will need an array of scissors in your personal toolbox. This will include both curved and straight scissors (and a back-up set), thinning shears, and other specialty scissors you will find that you love to use. You should invest in the best quality scissors you can afford because overall they can save you money. Good scissors are key to achieving precise and professional-looking grooms. Top quality scissors dull less often (if you take care of them) and you will save money by not having to pay to have them sharpened so often.

Buy more than one nail clipper. You may have a preference for which type of clipper you prefer (scissor or guillotine) but sometimes you need to adapt and adjust for the dog in front of you. Have at least one of each and possibly a backup.

BRUSHES AND COMBS

You should invest in several brushes and combs to cover an array of different breeds and assorted styles of cuts. There are different lengths of bristles for different types of fur. Combs also come in different sizes to suit different fur and different needs. There are also strippers (they're tools, not exotic dancers), dematting tools, and a host of grooming instruments which are all used to achieve different end results on different breeds that you should

Chapter 11.

have in your tool kit in anticipation of whatever breed appears on your grooming table.

ACCESSORIES
Alongside all of these implements, there are accessories that you need to have on hand. Ear powder, blade oil and cooling spray, hemostats for removing ear hair, flea removal supplies, soft muzzles, and a nail grinder set (Dremel) are the basic supplies every groomer should carry with them. Other highly recommended supplies you should buy are ribbons, bandanas, bows, and finishing sprays. Some of these may sound frivolous but are necessary to personalize your work. You will be limited without them and your work, and business, will likely suffer for that.

If you intend to start off as a subcontractor in someone else's grooming shop, you may find that the shop will provide some of the supplies listed above. Check whether they do or do not before accepting a job offer.

Keep all your tools and equipment in good repair. Upgrade them when you can afford to and when you find items that help you improve your work.

GROOMING ROOM EQUIPMENT
In addition to items in your personal toolbox, to professionally groom you will need to buy, or have access to, a few pieces of equipment and supplies. If you are working as a subcontractor in someone else's shop, you can reasonably expect the following items to be provided by the establishment. If you are operating your own shop, you will need to purchase them.

BATHING TUB
No dog, or cat, can be properly groomed until they are clean.

If you are the one investing in the tub, here is a word to the wise: buy the best, newest tub you can afford; yes, the one with all the bells and whistles. They are designed to make bathing easier and less physically stressful. Buy the ramp. Add the extra lift. Purchase the shampoo dispensers. Your back will thank you for it!

But if you cannot afford a top-tier tub with all the bells and whistles, do not despair. Buy the grooming tub you can afford. Your clients will never know and do not care. Buy the tub that you, and your back, actually want as soon as you can afford to.

A NOTE ABOUT BATHING TUBS: For the welfare of your entire plumbing system, you should seriously consider investing in a grooming tub with superior fur traps and filtration. This is particularly crucial if you are grooming from home. Pet fur is extremely damaging to plumbing and septic systems.

If you cannot afford a professional grooming tub (and the necessary new plumbing) or have no room to install one, you can bathe in a large utility sink or bathtub with a shower wand. Be extremely, even fanatically, careful to keep fur from going down the drain. Invest in multiple traps and keep them clean.

GROOMING TABLE WITH HOOKS AND LOOPS
Some groomers purchase their own folding/travel grooming table even if they work for someone else. They like the feel of their particular table. But if you work in someone else's shop, you can expect to be provided with a safe, well-maintained table with an apparatus to secure dogs for their safety. Anything less than safe should be a warning flag about that shop.

For your own shop, invest in a good quality table. It should be stable and strong enough to safely support all but the absolutely largest dogs on it.

Chapter 11.

STAND DRYERS

Do not try to save a few dollars by using a human hair dryer. They are not suitable. Period.

Every table in your shop needs its own professional-quality stand blow dryer. If you are a one-person business and only have one table, you only need one stand dryer. But if you can afford to, buy two. Having two dryers blowing on a heavy-coated dog can save you a lot of time and in grooming, time is money.

If you are opening your own shop and intend to hire other groomers to work for you (or rent space from you), you will be expected to provide them with their own table and their own dryer.

Buy the best stand dryers you can afford. Used dryers often come on the market and a secondhand stand dryer, if they are not too old and have been well-maintained, can last you for years.

CAGE DRYER

While not absolutely necessary, a cage dryer can be a great investment. While some dogs must be brushed the entire time their fur is drying, in order to achieve the desired result, not all dogs do. The latter can dry in a crate while you work on a second dog, which is a far more efficient use of your time.

Another reason for investing in a cage dryer is that there are dogs that cannot stand for long periods of time on a grooming table. Allowing them to take a break without sacrificing drying time is also a time saver.

You could use a second stand dryer to cage dry, but dryers specifically designed to attach to crates, generally, are worth the expense.

CRATES OR CAGE BANK

If you choose to schedule your clients so that there is only one pet on your premises at a time, you can probably get by with a single crate where you can secure your customer's pet as you get organized or while you wait for the dog's owner to come and collect their freshly groomed pet.

Realistically though, there will be more than one animal at a time in your care so you will need some sort of enclosures to keep those pets safe and out of trouble while you work. You will need crates or a cage bank.

Having a professionally built cage bank of several units is a terrific way to maximize your time, resources, and space. One dog can be cage drying while you bathe another, while a third dog sits in a separate crate awaiting its turn. Once a dog is completely groomed and ready to go home, they can wait in a clean crate with little risk of messing up all your hard work.

TOWELS

There are never enough towels in a grooming shop. Never. You will need loads of them. This is one item where used is as good as new. You can save a lot of money by asking friends to donate their old towels to you. Or buy them second hand from thrift shops.

WASHER AND DRYER

You will want to be able to *conveniently* wash and dry towels and other fabrics like aprons, because you will be doing laundry every day. Try to avoid washing grooming towels in your home washing machine; these towels are full of fur which you do not want clinging to your personal laundry or clogging up your home plumbing.

Remember to keep the filters of your washer and dryer free of fur by cleaning the filters and hoses out constantly; at least daily.

Chapter 11.

Depending on where you live, you may be able to minimize the use of a dryer and just hang dry your grooming towels. The upside to that is the savings and the sun sterilizes. The downside is that it takes longer and even the sunniest of locations has cloudy days.

SLIP LEADS

Customers may carry their pet into your facility without a leash. You will want to have a slip lead at the ready to ensure that their dog does not accidentally escape (it might be their fault but you could be held liable).

Another reason for having a few slip leads on hand is that it is common for a dog to need to relieve itself while in your care. A slip lead comes in handy to be able to take the dog out without messing up a finished groom by getting a collar on and off.

SHAMPOOS AND CONDITIONERS

Ideally you should have access to an array of shampoos and treatments. Different coats need different shampoos to optimize their condition. Some pets have allergies and need shampoos that do not aggravate their condition. And some clients simply despise certain smells so you will want to avoid those when you can. Shop around for good deals but go with brands you can trust from suppliers you can trust.

PEST TREATMENTS AND PROPHYLACTICS

Pets often come in for a groom with fleas or ticks. In fact, this is often the very reason a pet is brought in for a groom. You need to get rid of these parasites from the animal while at the same time prevent an infestation in your shop.

There are many topical and oral products in the market for you to choose from. But be aware that some are highly toxic and should be used with extreme caution. Also be aware that certain breeds carry genes that make them susceptible to extreme reactions to common treatments. Learn about any pest treatments thoroughly before you use them. Do not rely on sales reps; check with your local veterinarian regarding the use of parasite treatments or preventatives.

COLOGNES, PERFUMES, AND SPRAYS

Some groomers love finishing off their work with a spray of cologne, others do not. Some clients love getting their pet back smelling of perfume, others do not.

Since colognes and finishing sprays are cosmetic only, do or do not; it's up to you and your clients' preferences.

FIRST AID SUPPLIES

Accidents happen. When you work with sharp scissors and blades, they happen more often. Occasionally a groomer will nick a customer's pet; a groomer may cut themselves, or get bitten, or scratched. Make sure there is a fully stocked first aid kit available at all times.

Do not assume that human first aid products are suitable for animals. Except in the most extreme circumstances or with a vet's approval, use human first aid products for humans and animal first aid products for animals.

CLEANING TOOLS AND SUPPLIES

Even if your facility has a third-party cleaning service, you should have cleaning supplies on hand to clean up messes that cannot wait. Use professional grade products but be sure they are not toxic to animals.

Remember that the health and welfare of each animal you accept into your facility falls on you. Do all it takes to keep your facility clean, germ-free, and free from parasites. Make your shop a safe place for them and for you, your co-workers, and your employees.

Chapter 11.

VARIOUS BUSINESS MODELS FOR GROOMERS

There are various business models available for professional groomers. You can open your own brick-and-mortar shop or work out of a mobile grooming van, work from home, or work in someone else's shop. You could work for a breeder, a boarding kennel, pet supply store, or a vet clinic. Combining any of the above is also a possibility. Here is a list of options and what each requires:

<u>WORK IN SOMEONE ELSE'S GROOMING SHOP</u>

Many established grooming business owners hire additional groomers to work in their shop. This might be a great option for a new groomer who needs the income immediately and, perhaps more importantly, the experience. An established shop looking for an additional groomer obviously has more clients than they can handle. For the groomer, there is little risk, certainly minimal financial risk, to this business model option.

This may sound as if you are not actually starting your own business by working for someone else. However, "hiring" a groomer often means allowing a self-employed, independent groomer to work as a contractor in someone else's establishment. What are the positives and negatives for you?

On the one hand, as addressed, there is the lack of financial risk and virtually zero investment. You would be expected to arrive with your own personal tools but not the more expensive, heavy equipment such as stand dryers, tables, and tub. There is no rent to pay. Most shops will provide supplies like shampoos and ribbons, colognes and bandanas. They also provide the clients, saving you the expenses and the work of marketing. They will provide you with front office services such as handling reservations, collecting payments, and advertising. You will probably be expected to clean up your workstation, but the heavy cleaning of the shop is on them, as are the cleaning and disinfecting supplies.

In exchange for all that, they will take a percentage of your fees. Fifty or even 60 percent may sound like a lot but consider how much overhead they have in rent, utilities, supplies, and front and back office services that they are providing you. They are also providing you with clients and their good name. On your own, you would be covering all those costs while building a customer base.

As an independent contractor you will need to track your own income (though most shops provide comprehensive printouts of all your earnings), and you will be responsible for paying your own taxes and having your own insurance.

For those looking to groom without investing the time, money, or effort of owning their own shop, another great option is working for a veterinary practice or boarding kennel instead of a grooming shop. If your local veterinarian does not yet offer grooming services, consider speaking with them about adding them to their menu of services, with you as the provider of course. This could be a secondary source of income for the practice with a relatively small investment on their part.

In a like manner, many boarding kennels offer, or want to offer, grooming services. This would increase their revenues while providing a service, and added value, for their clients. Your relationship with the kennel would be similar, if not identical, to one you would have with a grooming shop. They provide the big items, you provide the labor and your expertise. They take a cut of your fees, you leave the risk and clean up to them.

Finally, there is another model for working in someone else's shop; that is to "rent" a table. You would pay the owners of the facility a fee and in exchange, that workstation is yours. The rent will likely include access to dryers, crates, and the grooming tub. The shop will expect you to find and book your own clients but may offer you "walk-ins". You would be responsible for setting your fees and collecting payments. The upside to this model is that all your income is your own.

<u>WORK FOR YOURSELF OUT OF YOUR HOME</u>
If you want your grooming business to be completely yours, a *relatively* low-investment option is to work from home.

Before embarking on this path, you should check with your local authorities regarding licensing and the legality of running any business from your home. There may be ordinances restricting this. You may need a special license to operate from a residence.

Costs for setting up and maintaining an in-home grooming shop may be low relative to setting up in a free-standing shop, but there are both upsides and downsides to consider.

Working from home saves on one of your biggest expenses: rent. Not only will you have no additional rent to pay, as you would if you opened a free-standing shop, but you may be able to deduct your home-based grooming room as a business expense. You should discuss this with a CPA or an IRS representative.

No one expects a home-based business to invest in signage or even a clever name. Eliminating either of these is a savings. But there are still items you will have to invest in.

You may be able to use an existing household tub, but if you have the space, a grooming tub is a better option.

You will need to buy at least one grooming table and one professional stand dryer. You will need stacks of towels, supplies like shampoos, bandanas and bows. Purchasing cleaning supplies and equipment is entirely your responsibility and expense. You will need to buy a crate or two to hold pets waiting to be groomed or waiting to go home. And you will need to designate enough room in your home to house all these items as well as enough space to work.

Like any pet care business owner, you will need to invest in business software to track your income and expenses, and it falls to you to run the business end of things.

Another downside to a homebased grooming business is that many customers will expect your prices to be lower than a "proper" grooming shop. This may take time to overcome. You might have to overcome the perception that you are doing this as a hobby.

Perhaps the biggest challenge as a business owner working from home is being able to separate work from home life. It is all too easy to let the business take over your life, especially when you are first starting out and building a customer base.

While you will not want to turn away new customers and will not want to say "no" to existing customers, do your best to set boundaries and stick to them. Except for true emergencies, and in grooming there are very few true emergencies, when you are booked you are booked and when you are closed, you are closed. Grooming "just one more dog" when you are tired may result in a subpar outcome, and that can tarnish your reputation. It is better to appear to be so in demand (even if you aren't) that clients need to wait a few days or weeks. This can work in your favor by improving your reputation, increasing your status, and encouraging customers to prebook their next appointment in advance. This is an enviable situation that allows you to justify raising your prices.

With all that, don't overlook the upsides to this business model. Besides not having to invest in a shop, working from your home has its advantages.

- There is no commute.

- When you are not actually grooming you can take care of things around your house and even do errands.

- By not committing to someone else's business, you can set your own schedule.

- Your marketing has a built-in hook. Create a narrative where the small size of your operation is its advantage and that your personal attention is added value to your clients.

- Every decision is yours to make. You get to choose which shampoos and other supplies you want to use or promote (and perhaps sell). You get to choose which pets you will and will not groom. You set your policies and prices.

BRICK-AND-MORTAR SHOP OR A MOBILE GROOMING VAN
The reason these two business scenarios are combined here is because at their core, they are more similar than different. They both require a large investment from the business owner. A brick-and-mortar shop will likely either have a mortgage or rent; a mobile van will have either a rental fee or vehicle loan. Both require you invest in *all* the heavy and light equipment and tools as well as all the supplies. Both have utility bills (electricity for both and gas for the van). Both require proper zoning, business licenses, license to occupy and operate. In the case of a mobile van, you will also need a license to drive. This is a huge commitment.

Yet, each of these work environments offer you independence and the most flexibility to expand your business and revenues. In each of these types of businesses you have an opportunity to hire additional groomers (reaping a portion of the fees they generate); rent out your facility (during hours or on days you do not want to groom); and usually can reach a wider market or customer base.

In your own shop, you can maximize your efficiency by taking on apprentices and bathers. You can increase revenues and your client base by hiring contracted groomers. You get to set the percentage you will take from each groom they do. Even if your shop is small and not suited for more than one groomer at a time, you can always come to an arrangement for another groomer to work on your days off when your space is empty and the equipment is idle.

If you decide you want to bring on additional groomers, be sure you have a clear understanding of what you expect from them and put that in a written contract. You may agree to manage the business end of things such as the marketing of the business, booking clients, collecting payments, and reporting income. You could also simply provide space for independent groomers who are responsible for their business and pay rent to use your facility regardless of the number of clients they groom.

Mobile vans typically do not have room for a second groomer. However, just as you can realize income from a groomer working in your brick-and-mortar on your days off, it is possible to rent your van to another groomer on the days you choose not to work. A grooming van sitting in your driveway generates no money.

If you rent out a mobile van, whether you charge by the hour or day or if you take a percentage of their fees, you should invest in a top-quality contract (an attorney is not a luxury but a necessity).

Chapter 11.

Do not skimp on your insurance and mandate anyone using your van, or grooming shop, have equally good insurance.

Final word about brick-and-mortar set ups: Be 100% sure the location you have chosen is zoned properly for a grooming shop *before* you sign a lease. Work with a reputable Realtor and an attorney. Have a trusted professional inspect and sign off on the plumbing and electrical capabilities to handle the heavy load of grooming equipment as well as a reliable HVAC unit.

FINAL BUSINESS MODEL: SPECIALIZED GROOMING

There are opportunities for you to groom where the money is good, extremely good even, but the customer bases are phenomenally small and highly selective. Did I mention the money is good?

1. Grooming pets that work in the entertainment industry. Just as actors have makeup artists and stylists, animals in entertainment or on the show circuit have "their people". This is a very difficult arena to get into. The owners or trainers of these professional pets often do the grooming themselves. But some can find themselves over extended or simply prefer to focus on the training and contract out the grooming. You will have to first build yourself a stellar reputation and have a lot of connections before anyone in the industry will entrust their animals to you.

You may need to relocate to a large metropolitan area to be able to create a sustainable business in this niche market.

If this area of grooming interests you, create an outstanding portfolio and reach out to talent agencies and trainers.

2. Grooming for dog shows.
Most owners of dog show competitors groom their own
dogs. But some can't or can't keep up and will hire a
professional groomer to help.

To groom show dogs, get to the level of master groomer
for that breed and then reach out to breeders and handlers.

3. Farriers and Shearers.
This book would be remiss if it did not at least briefly refer
to the highly specialized groomers who shear sheep and
alpacas, and farriers who care for hooves, usually horses'.
These professionals are typically overlooked as
professional groomers, perhaps because they work out in
the field and their clients do not go home with a cute
bandana. But make no mistake, they are groomers and
their clients are happier and healthier after grooming.
These professionals are running serious businesses and
these businesses can be highly profitable.

A deep dive into farrier or shearing businesses is beyond
the scope of this book, though. What can be said is that
there is a shortage of talented, professional shearers and
farriers and because of that, they are in demand and
demand means profits. If you are interested in entering
these fields, contact a working shearer or farrier and see if
they will speak with you about their business. They may
offer to teach and mentor you.

MARKETING YOU AND YOUR BUSINESS
Regardless of which business model is the one for you,
you will need to promote yourself. Even if you work for
someone else, you will want to develop your own
customer base and your own following.

Portfolios
Groomers are in an enviable position to be selling a
service for which photos are not only easily available, but

are particularly appealing on social media. Even in old-school print ads, photos can be powerful proof of the quality of your work.

Take lots of photos. Take "before" and "after" shots. Use your photos to decorate your shop. Show new or potential customers your album when you meet them for the first time.

NOTE: *Never* disclose personal or private information about your clients, even accidentally, when sharing these photos. And be sure to get permission, in the form of a photo release, from your customers to use photos of their pets for commercial use if you plan to use photos on your website or any other promotional materials.

SOCIAL MEDIA
Social media is where your portfolio really comes into play. Schedule time at least once a week to update all your social media accounts. They should be interesting and engaging. And you should have a presence on as many social media platforms as possible.

Other opportunities to market you and your business include:

RESCUES
Working with local rescues and offering to groom their dogs for free is a great way to support their efforts and get known in your community. If you cannot afford to do all their dogs, commit to grooming one or two each month. In exchange for your free labor, ask the rescue to attach your business card to the collar of any dog or cat that you groomed when it is adopted.

From time-to-time make sure your local news stations know about the rescue and, of course, your relationship with them.

MEDIA RELATIONS

Offer to write a weekly column about pet care for your local newspaper. Local papers often struggle to fill their pages. They also struggle to pay their writers. If you are willing to work for free (in exchange for getting direct access to your local target market), they may welcome you with open arms. Provide free photos to go along with each article.

The same is true for local newscasts. Offer to let them shoot a piece in your shop but also be willing to visit their studio. Have a long list of potential topics on which you have something to say ready to go.

Podcasts: Offer to be a guest on local or topical podcasts. In fact, why not start your own podcast? You could speak about products. You could address concerns many listeners and viewers (pet owners) share such as flea or tick prevention or blocked anal glands.

If you do not feel ready to go all-in with a podcast, write a blog. Become the go-to blogger for all things grooming- or pet care-related.

COUPONS AND DISCOUNTS AS MARKETING TOOLS

It can be tempting, especially when you are just starting out, to offer coupons and discounts in order to bring in new clients. This can be a useful tool in your arsenal, but it can also seriously backfire if not used prudently.

There are people who will "shop the coupons." That is, they are looking for the cheapest groomer and will only book with you when you offer them a discount. They will not be loyal. You cannot count on them as someone in your long-term client base. Their dogs tend to go for long periods of time without getting properly groomed (or brushed at all) and you will have to put in far more work for less money. Getting a reputation as a discount groomer will bring you discount clients. [Unless your goal is to be the cheapest groomer in town, you want to do all you can to keep your prices as high as the market will bear. At the very least, you want to be competitive. Why work for a $25 fee if you can groom the same pet for $50?]

However, incentives can be a positive thing if used judiciously. There is one very good time to offer discounts and coupons and that is during your slow periods. After a couple of years in business, you will start to see patterns of what constitutes your busy season and when your shop goes quiet. You will likely notice that May and June are extremely busy as families get their pets ready for summer. Then during the first two weeks of July your bookings drop off. Similarly, November and December may be the season during which you are booked to the max for weeks. Then suddenly, there will be a noticeable drop-off. Those lulls would be the time to drum up a little business and invite newcomers into your shop. It is better to take smaller fees for a limited time, than not have any income at all.

The key is to protect your brand while offering small incentives.

OTHER REVENUE STREAMS TO CONSIDER
Once your business is successful you may have the time or simply the drive to expand. You could add services unrelated to grooming such as pet sitting or dog walking. Or you could increase your reach with any number of complementary enterprises.

GO BIG
If you decide you want to expand and build a grooming empire, you could work toward opening additional locations. These could be owned by you or franchised. To do this, you should first gain the expertise and name recognition to justify others investing in you. You should also expand your business know-how by taking additional

business courses and spending time understanding what running multiple business sites (or franchises) entails. Speak with attorneys who work in this field.

ADD RETAIL

Adding a retail shop can increase your income, with relatively little additional work. The key word here is "relatively". You may not have room, or time, for a full-blown retail shop, but you could sell a few small items like brushes or combs or other pet grooming supplies. You could launch your retail store by setting up a small display in a corner of your shop and have a few boxes with inventory in a closet. With success, you can always expand to include larger retail space and fully-stocked warehouses, even if that means hiring staff.

Opening an online, or e-commerce, store eliminates the need for retail space and may even eliminate the need for you to stock inventory. However, while most e-commerce is handled automatically, it does require attention. This may be something you can manage in the evenings and your days off.

In real life or online, only sell those products that reflect your brand and that you would be proud to be associated with.

DEVELOP YOUR OWN PRODUCT LINE

If you are crafty and creative, you could make your own bows and bandanas and sell them to clients or other groomers. This is something you can do between clients, on your days off, or in the evenings. You could even recruit family members and friends to help.

Likewise, you could develop a line of products that could be produced to your specifications in a local or distant factory. Your products, your branding.

Chapter 11.

If you are working full-time as a groomer, keep your product production manageable and manage your expectations. Product development takes time and there is a lot of competition.

If you are interested in developing new grooming products, check out Chapter 13 for how to build a successful pet product business. As many products as there already are on store shelves, there always seems to be room for more.

TEACHING
Once you have the expertise, you can teach future professional groomers, or you could offer intimate, mini-classes to non-professionals who want to learn how to trim their pets' nails or how to maintain their dog between professional grooming appointments.

You can also teach related, but non-grooming, topics such as Pet CPR.

The sky's the limit for content. Just be sure your content reflects your brand. And be sure you are truly competent and experienced enough to teach the content you promise.

YOUTUBE OR OTHER SOCIAL MEDIA CONTENT CREATOR
Besides those wanting to learn to groom, there are people who simply love to watch groomers at work. Share your work live or recorded. Once you acquire a large enough viewership, income will follow.

SPECIALIZE
Since finding a groomer willing to take on cats can be a challenge for cat owners, *you* can be the "cat groomer" in your area. Or you could choose to become more than just proficient in grooming a specific breed or two of dogs. Create a "look" for your clients; a modified cut that will set you apart from your competition.

If you find that you have a flair for working with particularly challenging pets, market yourself as specializing in rescues, trauma victims, aggressive pets, etc.

Be sure you can deliver on what you promise.

BITS AND PIECES FOR PROFESSIONAL GROOMERS

- Try to meet your customers' wishes but never endanger the health of a dog or cat to achieve an unreasonable whim.

- Learn all you can about the products you are using. Just because it says "hypoallergenic" does not make it so. Do your own research. Find sales reps you can trust and work with them.

- If you decide to sell retail products, check with your local tax authorities about collecting sales tax (in some jurisdictions, service providers do not charge sales tax, but product retailers do).

- Look for opportunities to improve your skills and learn new ones. If you cannot find these opportunities, create them yourself.

- Try to give every animal a chance, regardless of its history. But know that sometimes it is better to pass a particular client on to someone better suited.

Chapter 12.
FOUNDING A SUSTAINABLE PET RESCUE

Flexibility: Low

Investment level: Extremely low to extremely high

Startup costs: As little as $0 to hundreds of thousands of dollars

Mandatory education: None

Recommended education: Pet CPR, pet behavior classes, basic bookkeeping, familiarity with rules and regulations governing non-profits

Necessary equipment: Smartphone

Recommended equipment: Depending on the type of animals you will be rescuing and/or rehoming: quality leashes, other devices to safely move animals from place to place, enclosures (crates, cages, stalls, paddocks, etc.), laptop, tablet, or desktop computer, access to transportation vehicles

Legal requirements: Non-profit tax status certification, necessary business licenses and permits, animal control compliance and licensing as needed, tax reporting accounts, insurance

THE FIRST RULE OF ANIMAL RESCUE
Before taking a look at any of the specifics of building and maintaining an animal rescue, we would be remiss if we did not stop and articulate clearly the first rule of animal rescue and that is: You cannot save them all.

If you try to achieve this impossible goal, you will fail.

If you cannot accept this rule, you will not emotionally survive this journey.

But, by combining your dedication with good business practices, you can create a working, sustainable pet rescue that can do a lot of good and save a lot of animals.

RESCUES FOR CARE; CARE FOR RESCUES

There are many different reasons why animals come into rescue and then need to be rehomed or provided for for the rest of their lives. The worst is when they are rescued from intentionally abusive situations. Another reason, perhaps less abhorrent, that some animals come into rescue is due to bad situations stemming from ignorance or bad planning. There are also rescued pets that need help through no one's fault such as when a pet owner dies or an animal gets loose accidentally and the owner cannot be found.

Domestic pets are not the only animals that need and enter rescue care. Many wild animals come into rescues following an illness or injury having been found by a Good Samaritan. Other wild animals need rescue as a result of poaching or hunting that leaves younglings without parents. And there are animals that are confiscated and rescued from illegal (and immoral) trafficking of exotic animals. Some of these animals are able to return to the wild after rehabilitation; others are destined to remain in the rescue's care in sanctuaries.

Whatever the reason, whichever the species, without rescues these animals would continue to suffer and would likely not survive for long.

And neither will your rescue if you don't treat it as a business.

There are three main challenges facing all rescues.

Chapter 12.

- How to rehabilitate traumatized animals during temporary care.

- How to place them in forever homes or sanctuaries (or return them to the wild) where they can live their best life in peace and security.

- How to stay in business so you can go on rescuing.

Most rescues are non-profits. Non-profit does not mean "no money". It merely means that the tax authorities recognize that your mission is for the greater good and will allow tax exemptions to help you achieve the organization's mission. Unlike for-profit businesses, the goal is not the bottom-line. The goal is to attend to your mission.

Keep in mind that there is no rule that says rescues have to be non-profit. But if you decide to create a for-profit rescue, you should make that status clear to any donors you may have. Their "contributions" would probably not be considered a deductible charitable contribution.

At the business level, the differences between for-profit and non-profit are as follows:

- At the end of the year a non-profit cannot be distributing dividends no matter how much money is in the bank. The goal of for-profit businesses is to make money for the owners and investors and of course to help animals in need.

- Use of the non-profit's money is highly regulated. For-profit companies can do as they please with their funds (absent illegal activity).

- You cannot sell a non-profit organization as you could a for-profit business. You do not "own" a non-profit organization, you run it. Alternatively, if you own a for-profit business, it is yours to run, sell, or close at will.

- Beyond having to be in compliance with animal protection laws and regulations, non-profits must comply with many rules, regulations, and reporting guidelines to prove and maintain their non-profit standing. For-profits just need to provide legal goods or services and to pay taxes.

Notice that nothing has been said about a non-profit not paying the founder a respectable salary or not paying its employees a living wage. Non-profits are allowed to provide for their workers. In fact, to be sustainable, you should be prepared to pay market-rate salaries.

Many people, with the best of intentions, get involved with rescues (or other non-profits) and think that every dollar they take as salary is a dollar that could have been better spent on the animals. Or that anyone who wants to help should volunteer their time and talent. That is a noble attitude, but it is not sustainable.

Unless you are independently wealthy, you need to earn a living so you can go on helping animals in need. So do your employees. It is great to have volunteers, but few people can afford to work full-time for no money. As the manager of a non-profit, you do not want to repeatedly have to train volunteers to replace those who have left you to earn a salary elsewhere.

On the flip side, and sadly, there are non-profits that pay their upper management as though they are running for-profit companies. The cause they are mandated to support comes after they take a hefty cut of donations, the very donations their staff worked very hard to secure. Don't be like them.

There is a happy medium.

Chapter 12.

Include in your budget fair-market wages for both you and your staff. Be in a position to do the good you set out to do long-term. In fact, all the decisions and plans you make should be with sustainability and longevity in mind.

Now let's see what it takes to create a framework for saving as many animals as possible.

THE BUSINESS END OF AN ANIMAL RESCUE

Animal rescues are, for the most part, non-profit organizations. Having non-profit status allows donors to write off donations as a tax deduction. This is a benefit that corporate donors are looking for. It is a bonus for individuals who choose to support your cause. The non-profit status also allows the rescue to avoid paying most taxes leaving more of those hard earned donations to be used for the mission. But it is here that the differences between for-profit and non-profits end.

Just as for-profit companies need a business plan, so will your non-profit.

- How will you raise awareness and then attract donors and supporters? You need a marketing plan.

- Your rescue's business plan needs to address the organization's expenses and how you plan to cover the costs of your overhead. Rent, utilities, and salaries all need to be paid. Rescued animals need to be housed, fed, and cared for. Vet bills can be costly, even at discounted rates. Your organization needs a budget.

- Your rescue needs to be focused with achievable and demonstrable goals. Your business plan needs to define the organizations mission statement, action items, forecasts, bios of each principal, and a budget.

This may sound exactly like creating a for-profit business. And they are similar. But pay close attention to the differences. They are crucial.

ESTABLISHING A NON-PROFIT ORGANIZATION VS. FOR-PROFIT BUSINESSES

You will need to:

- Create a business entity (just as you would for a for-profit company) but in accordance with non-profit rules and regulations.

- Apply for non-profit status from your tax authorities (very different from setting up an LLC or other business entity).

- Set up a bank account that is appropriate for a non-profit. These are not the same as regular business bank accounts. Your bank will require proof of non-profit status.

- Bring together a Board of Directors (For-profit entities may choose to have a BoD, but they are not mandated as they are for non-profits). These should be people who are committed to your mission and who bring "something" to the table. Some might have experience with other non-profits and can advise you based on that experience. Others may have animal husbandry experience and can help your work on the ground. Other board members may be well-connected in your community or have experience dealing with government entities and regulations. Large donors often insist on joining BoDs so they can help oversee the money they have donated.

- Write a set of bylaws. For-profits should have protocols and procedures, but they are not as legally mandated as bylaws are for non-profits. It is recommended that you get an attorney to help with writing your bylaws. Ideally, get an attorney who is committed to your mission who will do this work for free and who may even agree to sit on your Board of Directors, or at least advise you and your BoD.

Once you are established, your fiduciary (financial) obligations are different from those connected with for-profit businesses.

- Your bookkeeping must be impeccable so that you never risk losing your non-profit status. Establish protocols for all money in and money out. For instance, it is not uncommon for non-profits to require two signatures on large checks. This helps ensure good financial oversight. Get a CPA. Try to recruit one who will work pro bono, if you can.

- Unlike individuals and even some businesses, non-profits cannot "forget" to file taxes. Even though your organization is tax exempt, you need to file your tax returns. While other entities that fail to file their taxes can be fined, failure to file as a non-profit can result in not only being fined, but also losing your non-profit status.

WHERE TO SET UP YOUR RESCUE
Depending on the type of rescue model you choose, as well as the species you plan to help, you may or may not actually house the animals in your care in your home or on your site. If you do, check all your local ordinances for housing animals before getting in too deeply. It is one thing to take on a single foster dog or cat. Your property owner may mind but no governmental agency will get involved. But if you are housing multiple animals, or unusual animals, at your home, restrictions may exist and you need to know how to comply with them. This is *not* a

situation where asking for forgiveness is better than asking permission. You could find yourself scrambling to rehome animals just to avoid paying fines or face the confiscation of the very animals you were rescuing. Once you have connected with the appropriate authorities (health department, animal control), stay connected. This way you will know you are always in compliance.

At some point you may either outgrow your home-based rescue or you may plan to start out in a facility and never work from home. Be sure to confirm that any property you buy or rent is zoned properly for the types and number of animals you plan to house there. Work with experts as well as the authorities to be sure that what you build -and how you build it- is suitable for the animals in your care.

Your organization may choose to house your rescues in foster homes from day one. Or the animals you want to save may live on a completely different continent from where you live. Under those circumstances, you will need staff and/oversight wherever your rescued animals are, but where you set up your headquarters is far less important.

MARKETING A RESCUE
For-profit businesses generally have one marketing goal and that is to sell their service or product. Rescues have two narratives and each needs to reach the public. They may overlap, but they are different.

The first marketing mission is to raise awareness about your cause. By educating the public about the animals in need, you may reduce the number of animals you need to rescue. If cats are overpopulating your area, educating cat owners to spay or neuter their pets can impact those numbers. If your mission is to rescue abused dogs, educating the public about how to identify and report abusers can improve the situation and lessen the number of abused dogs. The irony is: the better you do your job, the more quickly you could put yourself out of business! Educating the public can be the best use of your funds since caring for rescued animals takes a lot more money.

The second marketing mission is to raise funds to support the animals that need rescuing today. Awareness is great, money is better.

Your message for each mission may overlap, but they need to be tailored to suit each audience. Where and how you approach each target audience may also overlap.

Be prepared to spend a lot of time marketing both your cause and your organization and its needs.

<u>SOCIAL MEDIA</u>
It has been well proven that quality is preferable over quantity when it comes to social media, regardless of the platform. Engage your followers with stories; not all of them tearjerkers, please. Include just as many happy endings as not. Access and use visual content but post only those photos that best depict your work and the animals you help. Just showing outrageously egregious abuse can be as much, if not more, of a turn-off as it may motivate.

Because you want to meet your supporters where they are, post on as many social media platforms as you can handle successfully.

Protect your reputation and your good name by never posting anything that can come back to haunt you. Do not bad-mouth other rescues or rant about a person who was forced to surrender a pet. Be professional but engaging, but don't engage in any negativity or arguments. Use that "block" button whenever it is called for.

Always end each post with a call to action. That call to action should be to donate or volunteer; but mostly to donate.

WEBSITE
Build a website that not only informs but calls people to action. The number one action you want the viewer to take is to make a donation. Be sure there are plenty of opportunities on your site to easily click through and make a donation, just don't overdo it.

Provide potential volunteers with a way to easily reach you.

BLOG
A blog is a great tool for keeping your supporters updated and engaged. If you can write, do. If you cannot, find someone who can and ask them to be the official blogger of your organization. Initially, require all posts get your approval before going live. Once you have confidence in your blogger, give them more autonomy.

Schedule time to write (or edit) your rescue's blog, even if it's only once a month. Consistency is important.

Blog posts should be short and well written. Be sure to edit for typos as well as content.

Link your blog to all your social media accounts.

BUILD A COMMUNITY OF EVANGELICALS
"Friend-raise" before you fundraise.

Since it's impossible to be everywhere all the time, build a cadre of supporters who are as passionate as you are about the animals you want to help. They can help you fundraise. Instead of having to solicit each dollar you need, allow your 'evangelicals' to share the burden for both fundraising and awareness-building.

ESTABLISHING THE NUTS AND BOLTS
Now is a good time to remind you of the fundamental axiom of animal rescue: you cannot save them all. You may want to and that is very noble. But there will always

be just one more out there. Your mental and emotional health, and your ability to sustain yourself and your rescue organization, depends on you internalizing this fact. For your rescue to survive, you must set boundaries and stick to them. Remind yourself how many animals will not be helped if, in your effort to save them all, your rescue does not survive. Then do the best you can.

<u>STARTING OUT</u>
A good rule of thumb for any rescue is to start small and scale up later. If you run before you walk it will be the very animals you are trying to help who may suffer the most. Take in one dog, rehabilitate and rehome her, and then take on another one. Build up to the maximum number you can handle at once and then stop. If you have room, time, and support for five cats, do not take on the sixth. Find alternative care for poor number six. Do not compromise the care for the five already in your rescue by over-extending.

<u>SET PARAMETERS AND BOUNDARIES</u>
Which animals do you want to rescue? What are your geographic boundaries? How will you house and care for the animals that make it into your rescue? What's the end game for each animal?

Chances are good that you already have a specie in mind. Although many rescues branch out (they start with rescuing goats and end up with an emu or two), focus on your target animals while the rescue is starting up and you are gaining experience.

Your rescue could be very specific and focus on a single breed of dog, cat, bird, or horse. This is very common. Most breed rescues will help find a solution for dogs of other breeds, but they reserve their resources for the dogs of their target breed. An upside to focusing on a specific breed is that some potential donors may share your passion for that specific breed and will connect with your narrative, and give money, because of that shared passion.

If you prefer to open your rescue to all dogs (or horses, cats, birds, or goats), that works too. There are plenty of generic animal lovers who will support you no matter what shape or size your rescued animals come in.

Don't forget to set geographic boundaries.

Sadly, you won't have to look very hard to find animals in need all over. But how far your organization can reach will impact, and be impacted by, your resources. Travel takes time, money, and personnel. Make sure you have all three before you commit. There are rescues with the funds and partnerships that can transport, even fly, animals into rescue care and eventually transport them to their forever homes. If your rescue can afford to do that, great! But even the best funded animal rescues have their limitations. Know yours.

That is not to say that you have to say 'no' to an animal in need just because they are out of your designated geographic area. It just means that maybe your resources are better spent by finding and teaming up with a sister-rescue closer to that animal in need.

Decide up front what the end game is. Are the animals in your care going to be released into the wild? Do they all need permanent 'forever homes'? Can your facility handle those who can never return to the wild or who never find their forever homes? You may not have answers for each animal but have a gameplan in place regarding how many you can keep long-term or forever.

Another area you need to set parameters and boundaries for is your free time. Rescue work can take over your life. Don't let it. Build in time for you and each of your staff and volunteers to take time for themselves.

Chapter 12.

How do you effectively bring a rescue animal in and how do you successfully rehome them? How can you track the care for your rescued animals if you don't have instructions as to what that care should entail?

By developing protocols and procedures, you and all your staff will know what to do, how and when to do it, and how to evaluate that it has all been done properly.

Intake protocols and procedures
Intake protocols and procedures include evaluating the animal in front of you but also include how you and your staff deal with all rescues coming into your care.

This is where your detailed record of this animal begins. Each animal brought into your rescue needs to have a detailed record that should follow this animal through rehabilitation, rehoming, and even beyond.

Create an intake form and insist it is filled out for each animal in your care, no matter how long or short that care takes. The record should include:

- photos of the rescue animal
- medical records, if available
- a history of how they came to you

Intake personnel must then evaluate the physical condition and mental or emotional temperament of each animal you choose to take in. Since most animals entering rescue are suffering from trauma (to various degrees), this is not the time to label them. This stage of the process is just to record initial observations so that anyone coming in contact with this newcomer is aware of the animal's specific immediate needs.

Intake protocols should also address any need for a quarantine or emergency medical care.

Have in place the necessary housing (and care supplies) for the animals you intend to care for. Crates or runs for dogs or cats. Cages for birds. Paddocks for horses. Have enough so that newcomers can decompress and acclimate in their own time and space and you can assess them before introducing them to your animals or other animals in your care.

Initial, short-term, and long-term care

Intake protocols and procedures must be standard for each animal. The care for each animal may vary. Short and long-term procedures and protocols need to be flexible enough to cover the needs for individual animals.

Your procedures governing on-going care should cover:

- Feeding (what and when)
- Grooming (when and how often)
- Training (when to begin)
- Exercise (alone or with others)
- Housing
- Rehoming (how to evaluate each potential adoptive family)

These need to be well-formulated by your team and experts and adhered to strictly by you and your staff. Foster families must commit and contract to follow them as well.

Foster families

There are several reasons a rescue may choose to rely on foster homes such as limited room at your facility, or the need for certain animals to be with fewer animals as they rehabilitate. A foster home is also a good way to prepare a rescue pet to transition from living in a facility to living with a family. Good foster care is often where the best rehabilitation takes place. Traumatized animals can learn to trust again, and they learn, or relearn, how to live in homes. Fosters are angels and need to be appreciated for the work they do, the time they spend, and the heart they give with absolutely no expectation of personal gain.

Foster families are not necessarily professionals. By establishing and providing instructions and guidelines, you can minimize a lot of misunderstanding and heartache. But even before that, you have an obligation to the animals in your care to find the right foster families. This can be done by setting standards and processes.

- Create a process for evaluating foster families. This is not a time to rely solely on your "gut feeling", though sometimes that can be the final deciding factor.

- Unless you know the candidates personally and well, do background checks.

- Even if you are friends with potential fosters, check their homes. Make sure the environment is safe for each animal. Carry out periodic spot home checks.

- Not every foster family is suited for every animal that comes into rescue. Have a system in place to assess the best candidate from your list of available foster homes for each animal.

Rehoming

Rescued animals have already suffered enough trauma; they deserve to be rehomed a minimal number of times. Unsuccessful rehoming can come down to one of two mistakes: a misevaluation of the animal or the misevaluation of the adopter. Finding the right match is an art, not a science. But having a rigorous and thorough evaluation process minimizes mistakes.

- Constantly evaluate the animals in your rescue. Do not rehome any animal until you have a solid understanding of its true temperament and personality. Knowing what environment is best suited for each is one of the best ways to find the right forever home. Remember that the initial intake evaluation may no longer be relevant once a rescued animal has been cared for and given the time to rehabilitate.

- Speak with more experienced rescues and your local animal control to learn what they use to evaluate adoption requests. See what they do and what questions they ask in their evaluation and application process. Develop yours accordingly.

- Create a detailed and thorough application form for prospective adopters. Create evaluation protocols and make home visits. Do not skip this process no matter what.

  If an applicant lives far from you, find someone near them whose opinion you can rely on and ask *them* to complete the home evaluation visit. One way to do this is to team up with other rescues and support each other. They need not be rescuing the same breed or even the same species necessarily. If your rescue works with Beagles, with a little guidance, a local rescue for Poodles can certainly evaluate the home and family wanting to adopt a Beagle in your care.

Fiduciary and business protocols and procedures
Strict protocols and procedures should govern every single aspect related to the finances of your rescue. This is not only to be in compliance with the tax authorities, but also to reassure your donors. These rules and guidelines will help reduce, if not eliminate, costly mistakes that might

otherwise be made by any well-intentioned employees, or yourself.

Fortunately, you do not have to reinvent the wheel. Most of the rules and regulations related to the finances of non-profits will have already been set by tax authorities and other government regulators.

Internally, you should establish additional ones specific to your organization. These might include but should not be limited to:

- who has access to the bank accounts or credit cards
- what spending limits are imposed and when two signatures are necessary for large outlays of money
- how petty cash and reimbursements are managed

Related internal protocols and procedures are needed to govern:

- Hiring and firing processes
- Vendor terms and conditions and the acceptance of tenders
- Expansion or other significant changes to the structure of the rescue

All internal procedures and protocols should be voted on and documented by your board of directors. They should then be disseminated to your entire staff and strictly followed. The rescue's financials should be reviewed regularly by the board of directors.

ENSURING YOUR RESCUE REMAINS SUSTAINABLE
To sustain an animal rescue for the long haul, you need to be attentive to two things: human resources and finances.

HUMAN RESOURCES
Burnout is your enemy.

Do not let the rescue take over your life, no matter how passionate you are about the mission. It is extremely easy to let your commitment take over your life to the exclusion of all else. That may even sound tempting. However, not only would that be unhealthy, but it is also not sustainable. No one can work ceaselessly for long, with no relief, and remain at the top of their game. You need to take time for yourself and recharge your batteries. You need to take care of you, otherwise, who will be there down the road to take care of the animals who are depending on you?

Pay yourself a living wage. Get health insurance. Medical insurance is an acceptable business expense and access to medical care is a basic human right. Allot yourself vacation days and take them! Find ways to relax outside of work. Have a life. The mission is important but so are you.

Do not let the mission burn out staff or volunteers, either. They deserve the same level of care that you do. Your protocols and procedures can go a long way toward doing that.

Create an employee handbook and include protections against misconduct and abuse. Set definitive salaries and clearly define work hours and vacations. Keeping your staff healthy is a key factor in ensuring that the work of the rescue hums along and does not sputter because workers are too tired to give 100%. Being attentive to your staff's needs can make all the difference, especially during busy or challenging times.

If you think that the cost to take care of your staff is too high, consider this: Finding, hiring, and training good employees is hard and it can be expensive. It is certainly a time-suck. The same is true for good volunteers. After putting in so much time and effort to train them, you will not want all your good work to be for nothing if they leave. Your biggest assets are your workers so make them feel valued and appreciated. Protect them. Pay them as well as you can. If you do all this, they will give more than 100%, they will have your back, and they will stay.

The same care and attentiveness you give yourself and your staff should be applied to the financial health of your organization.

FINANCIAL SOLVENCY
If your rescue goes broke, you will not be able to help anyone or anything. Profitability may not be the goal as it is in the for-profit sector, but solvency and sustainability are. Ensuring the financial health of your rescue organization comes down to two things: controlling expenses and maximizing revenues.

EXPENSES
Controlling expenses is a massive challenge. This does not mean that you need to rely 100% on volunteers or that you must go unpaid. It does not mean that animals need to go without the proper care they need and deserve. It means that you need to stretch every dollar you bring in and get creative in lowering your costs.

For instance, shop for supplies during the off-season or when they are on sale, or shop at second-hand outlets for items that do not need to be new for sanitary reasons. Towels can be second-hand as can stainless steel food dishes. Bedding, leads, or travel crates should not.

Buy in bulk when it makes sense. Buy pet food in bulk but then be sure to invest in top-quality storage bins to protect the food from vermin, weather, and oxidation.

Team up with other rescues or related organizations to secure lower costs. Insurance for a large number of people is almost always lower than for an individual.

Other ways to save include:

- Share expenses. If you transport your rescue animals, see if there are other rescues moving their animals at the same time in the same general vicinity and take one vehicle or negotiate a better rate from the transporter.

- Team up. Find a local vet who will treat the animals in your rescue at discounted fees. Offer to take in animals that are abandoned outside their clinics (it happens a lot) in exchange for their services. Do the same with other service providers such as kennels or trainers. Remember to thank your partners both privately and publicly. Support them in their businesses at full market rates whenever possible.

- Save where you can. Don't overlook saving on your utilities, social media costs, office supplies, and other regular bills; these can add up. Run the A/C if you need to but only as low as you absolutely must. Unless you are using your website to sell products, go for the least expensive hosting option. Save banking fees by finding the least expensive banking option. Be sure to use your tax exemption whenever possible. These savings may be small but they add up.

While not expense-related, here is some advice for the solvency of your rescue: Save for a rainy day.

Planning for the future is hard, especially when you are focused on the challenges of today. But it will go a long way to keeping your rescue viable for a long time if you can build a reserve fund. Commit to saving a small portion of each donation for future work and emergencies. Set up a second bank account if necessary; just be sure your financial statement includes this account. Non-profits are not obliged to use all their funds at once. They are allowed

to save for the future; they just need to report all their
funds in the bank to the tax authorities.

Which now brings us to the life-blood of all non-profits:
fundraising.

REVENUES

For any business, revenues and income are a never-ending
challenge. For non-profits that offer nothing tangible in
return, the challenge is greater.

Getting the money to create and then sustain any non-
profit is a full-time job. In fact, it is such a full-time job
and such a challenge that there is an entire industry of
professionals who do nothing but fundraise. Your rescue
could hire a third-party professional fundraiser, but they
can be very expensive. Their percentage comes off the top
before the first dollar enters your bank account; your non-
profit gets the residuals.

But do not reject using a professional fundraiser out of
hand. They may take a chunk of the funds, but some is
better than none and none is what you will get if you do
not have time to dedicate to fundraising.

Alternatively, you could hire a director of development as
an in-house fundraiser; but that person is going to expect a
salary. If you are lucky, you might be able to find a
professional who will agree to come on board to fundraise
for your rescue for a minimal salary, or even pro bono,
until such time that fundraising picks up. The upside to
having a director of development, rather than a third-party
professional fundraiser, is that they are dedicated to, and
focused on, your cause only. And their salary remains
constant no matter how much money they secure.

Most often though, in the startup phase, most CEOs or
founders of non-profits do their own fundraising. Donors
and supporters will not think less of your organization for

it. In fact, many donors appreciate the frugality of keeping staff to a minimum. And large donors want to be solicited by the person in charge anyway.

If you have never fundraised before, it might be intimidating. It is not easy to ask people to part with their money. But it's not brain surgery. Others have done it and you can, too. You will get better at it with practice.

To start to fundraise all it takes is a good cause (your rescue), a great narrative (the one you create for your business plan), an eye for opportunity (they are everywhere), and some creativity.

DIRECT DONATIONS
One way to secure funds is by direct donations. Basically, you draw up a list of potential donors by researching the likelihood of them supporting your rescue. You ask to meet with them. You explain who you are, what your cause is, what their money will go towards, and then ask for an amount of money. This can be done in person or through a phone appeal. Either way, it's called cold-calling. For most people, especially for those who have never done it before, it is uncomfortable.

If you are uncomfortable at first, write a script and practice in front of a mirror. Then practice with your friends. The script does not have to be complex - KISS (keep it super simple) - but it should be authentic. Let your passion show (but do not overdo it).

It might help if you think of this as *friend*-raising instead of fundraising. A one-time donation is great; a long-time supporter is better. Online campaigns tend to look for a one-time donation with the hope of converting donors to habitual supporters. Face-to-face solicitation can also result in a one-off donation, but that should be your fallback position. Go for the long-term support. Once you have a committed, long-term supporter, ask for their help

214

in reaching other potential donors in their sphere of influence.

IN-KIND DONATIONS

In-kind donations are those where money is not exchanged. A veterinarian who offers to treat the animals in your care for free or at a reduced fee is making an in-kind donation. So is a pet supplier donating food. Ask your website host if they have a special deal for non-profits. Do the same for any vendor you work with.

Saving on these expenses can be more efficient than having to raise the money these things would cost if not for the donation. You will be able to offer these supporters receipts for tax deductions for their businesses. And you can best repay them by promoting their businesses in return for their support.

SUPPORT FROM ORGANIZATIONS AND THE BUSINESS COMMUNITY

Many businesses and community groups are committed to doing charity work. They may supply volunteers, or they may be willing to underwrite some expense you have. Ask if a local civic group will cover your electric bill for a year or commit to one case of pet food a month. You might get lucky and find a CEO who is as passionate about rescue as you. They may offer support through their company by allowing their staff to get involved on company time. They might also become a long-term partner, a corporate supporter, and a donor.

FUNDRAISING EVENTS

Beyond approaching targeted individuals and groups to support your rescue, you can expand your outreach with slightly more fun ways to fundraise by holding public events. They are only "slightly more fun" because while it may be fun for participants, these events take a lot of work on your part.

The aim is for the event to cost you less than the amount you take in from selling entry tickets, raffle tickets, or auctioning donated items. If you do not walk away with money to put toward your rescue, all you have done is thrown a really good party, so make sure these events are money-makers.

Start small and don't bite off more than you can chew. Enlist friends and current supporters to help.

Here are just a few examples of simple fundraising events and funding sources. But don't limit yourself to these, get creative!

1. Old-school fundraisers
   Some bowling alleys will discount the cost to bowl for large groups and for non-profits. Ask if you can book their lanes for a closed event. Invite your friends and have them invite their friends.
   Advertise locally and maybe ask any local bowling league if their members would be interested in joining your efforts.
   The same can be organized at local craft businesses such as pottery glazing or group painting instruction.
   Your local movie theater may be open to arranging a special, private showing for your organization. They may even reduce, or even waive, the cost of the tickets so your guests pay the normal posted price, but your organization pockets the difference. These may be old fashioned but bake sales and car washes still work, too.
2. Dinners and galas
   When you are more experienced and adept, go for formal dinners and galas. The best way to make gala evenings profitable is to get as much of it donated as possible.

Consider honoring one of your big supporters, or honor several people at once, at the event. This is a sure-fire way to ensure they will invite their friends and family and fill the room (buying lots of tickets!).

If you plan to give out awards to your top donors, find a local awards shop that will donate (or greatly discount) some pretty, engraved awards. Instead of serving a full meal, serve hors d'oeuvres and find a local winery that will not only donate cases of wine they might choose to promote (win-win) but will also staff the bar.

Try to enlist donors to underwrite the entire event as their donation, then all the funds raised from the event go straight into the rescue's coffers. Large donors often like to do this because their single donation can result in a much larger bottom-line, many times larger than what they initially gave.

Besides traditional fundraising, there are sources for funding that go untapped every year, for instance, grants.

GRANTS
There are funds, sometimes a lot of funds, available for almost every mission known. And some of this money is in grant-form. Grants are blocks of money given with a specific use in mind and they can only be used for that purpose.

There are databases packed with names of people or groups willing to fund animal rescues through grants. The challenge is in getting chosen to be a recipient of that money.

Applying for grants generally costs nothing. There is usually an extensive application to fill out but once it is submitted, all you have to do is wait for the judges to choose from the hundreds if not thousands of applicants, each hoping to receive the very funds that you want to secure. Occasionally there is an interview process as well.

How can you increase your chances of getting selected? Hire a professional grant writer. This is one instance where hiring a professional is almost always better than doing it yourself.

Grant writing is an art. The applications can be long and tedious and to stand out you really need to know how to grab the attention of the processor. Professional grant writers do this. Some grant writers will agree to defer payment until (and unless) you win the grant. That is a great motivator and while you may not get the grant, you have not lost any money trying.

If you do become a recipient of a grant, leverage that fact in future applications and in all your marketing materials. Grant funds and institutional donors respect organizations that have previously been selected for grants. It raises their faith in you to know that others found you worthy and that you will wisely manage any money they give you.

SPONSORSHIPS
Sponsorships connect donors and supporters with a particular animal. This connection can become quite personal for these donors. This might require more work on your part as you will be expected to update each sponsor with news about the animal they are supporting. But in exchange for your extra work, hard to place animals, or animals with expensive veterinary treatments, can have their financial needs met directly without compromising the funding for the other animals in your care.

PASSIVE DONATIONS
There are companies and organizations that partner with animal rescues (and other non-profits) and support their selected nonprofits by fundraising on their behalf or by

matching donated funds. One example would be to team up with a local Scout troop or other community youth group looking for a community service project. The amount of work needed to arrange and even sustain such a relationship is far less than the work needed to actively fundraise or apply for grants!

LEGACY ENDOWMENTS
Your most passionate supporters may consider leaving your rescue money when they die, through legacy endowments. But this can happen only if you prepare the groundwork for such donations, and then ask for them. Work toward making all your supporters so passionate for your cause that they will leave your rescue money in their will.

ADOPTION FEES
It is common for rescues to charge a fee to adopt an animal from their care. It may seem counterintuitive to charge for an animal that so desperately needs a home. But there are two particularly good reasons to do this.

The first is to cover some of the money the rescue expended on caring for that individual animal and so that there is money available for the next one.

The second is that, sadly, without a monetary buy-in to weed out less-than-thoughtful adopters some rehomed animals will find their way back to a rescue situation.

THE SALE OF BRANDED MERCHANDISE
Putting your organization's name and your mission statement on a good quality T-shirt or other promotional item is a great way to not only raise funds but also to make your cause a household name.

Most customers ordering these items will already be supporters themselves or are friends and families of supporters. But never underestimate the power of a clever phrase or good-quality mug to raise funds from people who had never heard of you before! There is no need to invest in a storefront to do this. You can sell these items through your website or at community events.

If you are contemplating selling goods, be familiar with laws surrounding sales tax as a non-profit organization.

HOW TO GROW OR EXPAND YOUR RESCUE
You may start your rescue by taking in a few kittens or taking care of a single horse. Over time, a few becomes some, then some becomes a lot, and before you know it, you are maxed out and bursting at the seams. What do you do? How do you expand?

One way to expand your rescue is simply to expand your facility or add a secondary facility. If you have started in your home, taking on any facility will expand your operations. It may be an additional expense, but it will allow you to care for more animals in need.

Alternatively, instead of expanding or adding facilities, recruit an ever-growing cadre of foster families, which were discussed earlier. While this may not work with wild or exotic animals, this scenario works well with most domestic pets.

THIS BRINGS US BACK TO THE FIRST RULE OF RESCUE…
which is that you cannot save them all. Sadly, there will likely never be enough room, enough fosters, enough homes for every animal in need.

Aim high but just do your best with what you have. Remind yourself that you are doing the work of the angels, then do the best you can.

BITS AND PIECES FOR RESCUES
- Hire staff and pay them a fair wage. It's okay to take on volunteers to pull up the slack but relying

on unpaid labor for the long haul is not realistic nor sustainable. Pay yourself a fair wage, too.

- Friend-raise before you fundraise. It's more effective.
- Never co-mingle your money with money belonging to the rescue.
- Never compromise your non-profit status. Stay in compliance with the tax authorities.

Chapter 13.
CREATING AND SELLING PET PRODUCTS

Flexibility: Moderate

Investment level: Moderate+ to very high

Startup costs: From a few hundred dollars to hundreds of thousands of dollars

Mandatory education: None

Recommended education: Business management, bookkeeping and microeconomics; depending on the product: materials engineering, chemistry, food science, pet nutrition, pet psychology

Necessary equipment: This can range from a cutting board and a refrigerator, to a tool kit and workshop, to a fully outfitted production line and factory (depending on the product to be manufactured)

Recommended equipment: Depends on the scope of the business. An exclusive boutique product that wants to remain local might be sustainable with a small production line. A product that is intended for mass distribution will need a factory or access to a third-party manufacturer.

Legal requirements: Business entity, business license; certification from appropriate governmental health or product safety departments, ability to pay taxes across jurisdictions; insurance

WHY BECOME A PET PRODUCT MANUFACTURER
Besides the obvious "to make money", there are several reasons people choose to produce new or improved pet products. One common reason entrepreneurs undertake

this huge investment of time, energy, and money is they believe they have a way to improve on an existing product. This is how the market ends up with dozens, if not hundreds, of different variations of leashes, collars, cages, bedding, toys, and of course, food. Sometimes the improvement is in the materials or ingredients and sometimes it is in the design or price. Since consumers love to have options (up to a point), this is completely legitimate and feasible. In fact, letting others test the waters and then jumping in with a better version can be a wise business decision.

Innovation motivates others to develop completely new pet products. These entrepreneurs see a need that is not being met and they set out to find a solution in the form of a completely new product. A simple yet great example of this is leash couplers (to walk multiple dogs at once). One can imagine the developer being frustrated walking multiple dogs at once, the leashes getting tangled, and then looking for a solution. The solution was a simple attachment to link two collars to one leash.

Sometimes the need innovators and inventors are looking to fill is very personal. The pet "wheelchair" is a great example of this. The inventor, veterinarian Lincoln Parkes, saw the suffering of animals who had either lost limbs or were partially paralyzed and decided to help.

The third reason inventor-entrepreneurs create new products is to meet or anticipate changes in the existing market. Perhaps the best example of this is manufactured and packaged pet foods. Before the 1940s, house pets were generally fed leftovers, both raw and cooked. Then, seeing an entrepreneurial opportunity, manufacturers of human food began making and selling processed food for pets (and livestock). This was new, it was innovative, and it changed the pet ownership mindset. Fast forward to the mid-1980s when a raw-diet movement started. Entrepreneurs saw the interest in those dietary changes and began to manufacture raw diet products for pets.

Today, many of the innovations for the pet industry are tech-based devices. There is even a new moniker for this subsector: Pet Tech.

Whatever *your* motivation, be aware that this segment of the pet industry is highly saturated and has become very sophisticated. To make your product stand out, you will need to invest a lot of time, effort, and money; a lot of focus and drive; and have a bit of luck. Take time to do your homework and research the market and your product before you get in too deep.

BRINGING A PRODUCT TO MARKET

It cannot be overstated: Creating a product, bringing it to market, and then getting people to buy it takes research, time, trial and error, and nerves of steel. But first comes the research.

You need to know all there is about the current market and market trends. If you want to build a better mousetrap, you should know all there is to know about the mousetraps that are in stores currently. You need to know why they sell but also what they may lack. Learn why people do and do not like them. Then do better.

Do not marginalize the need to research your competition thoroughly and honestly. Do not dismiss them out of hand; after all, they are already selling, and you are not. Find out what they are doing right and consider what you would do differently with their product. Find out how they manufacture, package, and market their products. Think about how you can do better. Be honest with yourself about their strengths and your weaknesses.

Then research your own product thoroughly. Know all its ins and outs and intricacies, its strengths and its weaknesses. If your goal is to sell a better cat tree, make sure it is actually better. If your goal is to sell a cheaper water dish, find out not only what your competition sells theirs for, but how much it will costs you to manufacture your version; be sure it can be sold for less but still at a profit.

You must research your potential vendors and contractors all along your supply chain. You need to know every detail about every step in the production of your product including the price and sources of all your raw materials, the price of packaging and marketing; and who and where your sales outlets are.

It should go without saying that you must know who your actual target customers are. Sadly, many novice entrepreneurs do not. Your target market is never "everyone" and not even "everyone with a cat".

Let's say you are developing a new, healthy dog treat. You might be tempted to think that your target market is all dog owners everywhere. But that is unrealistic. Many dog owners never buy dog treats; some never give their dogs treats at all. Then there are those who may buy treats but would never pay what you would need to ask for your top-quality treat, so they are not your target customers either. There are dog owners who are loyal to brands currently in the market, so you will be hard pressed to convert them to customers. The list goes on and on and your target market gets smaller and more narrow.

Take the time to really define who your target market is and then calculate, or guesstimate, what small percentage of the multibillion-dollar pet treat industry you can realistically hope to convert to customers. If that number can support your efforts, you just might have a viable product.

Once you are confident that the market not only "needs" your product, but will also support it, it is time to create a prototype and beta test it.

CREATING AND PROTECTING A UNIQUE PRODUCT
Even before you go into production, if you have a new and unique product, protect it. The veterinarian who created the first pet wheelchair did not. Because of that, an identical design was patented by someone else. The patent holder, not the inventor, collects royalties.

LICENSING AND PATENTS
Licensing fees are monies paid to patent holders for the use of their patented products, processes, or designs. Whether or not you were first to create that new product, process, or design, it's only the patent holder who can approve a licensing agreement for their use by a 3rd party and it's only the patent holder who gets paid that licensing fee. So, patents can be valuable and are not something to be taken lightly.

Even if you think your product is unique, you must do research to determine that there are no existing patents governing any part of the product you want to develop or you may end up in court getting sued for patent infringement. If you find that yours is a unique creation, and is patentable and hasn't been patented before, apply for a patent to protect your investment.

It is possible to do your own patent search; the information regarding patents is publicly available. But consider the worth of hiring a patent attorney to search for you. Theoretically, each step in the process you are proposing could have already been patented. It could take weeks or months for a lay-person to do what an experienced patent research office can do in days.

What do you do if you find there is a patent on your product or one of its critical components? You can pay a licensing fee to the patent holder. This might set your teeth on edge, but you might have to do precisely that. Alternatively, you could create a new design that is different enough from the patented version to make your version patentable.

There is always the possibility you will not be allowed to patent your product. Not all products are patentable. And if you are only marginally improving on an existing product you may not be able to patent that. But it is definitely worth reviewing. If an attorney can secure you a patent that will ensure royalties for decades, that legal fee will be well worth paying.

REGULATIONS AND LIABILITIES

Taking an idea, even a great idea, through to production is a process. Before you get too far into that process, you must consider all the regulations and liabilities that can govern and impact your product. There is no point in investing time and effort into an item that won't meet governmental guidelines (and therefore cannot be sold) or that will come back to haunt you later in the form of lawsuits.

Most government guidelines can be found online or by contacting the various oversight agencies directly.

SAFETY

No one sets out trying to produce a faulty product, but it happens. You can, and almost certainly will, be held liable for damages caused by your product, especially if it is proven that you knowingly sold a subpar product. Retailers may never again take on a product of yours if they have

228

even once been burned by stocking a faulty product. Customers, particularly in the age of social media and public reviews, can destroy your business and reputation if your product is (or even appears to be) faulty or unsafe.

All consumer items are subject to review and can be recalled and pulled from shelves on an agency's say-so. Each country has its own government agencies that set safety guidelines. If you manufacture your product in one country and plan to import them to another, local agencies can block their importation.

The best way to combat these nightmare scenarios is to keep your standards high, from design through production. Learn what government and industry standards are and do better than that. Test and beta test until you get it right.

Remember, a pet's life could hang in the balance.

KNOW YOUR RAW MATERIALS

The importation of raw materials is subject to many of the same guidelines and rules that will govern the sale of your end product. So, not only should you source your raw materials carefully from good quality sources, but make sure they will pass governmental restrictions.

Ironically, food products for pets are fairly loosely regulated but are not exempt from all oversight. Regardless of quality or nutritional worth, it is possible to sell almost anything and call it pet food. But pet food that is found to be making animals sick, eventually face exposure and censure.

Beyond government oversight, be aware that consumer protection groups can, and do, speak out against products that were created from raw materials that came from what they deem to be questionable sources. Bad publicity will not do your bottom line any good.

<u>PRODUCTION SAFETY</u>
One final word about safety and that is, safety in the
production process. Many consumers will reject your
product, even before trying it, if they know that the
conditions under which it was manufactured was unsafe or
unfair. And consumers always find this out. Cutting costs
by using less expensive but substandard manufacturing
plants may seem like a good idea, but if this choice turns
off consumers, it will prove costly.

With all that in mind, if you are still all in, let's go.

CREATING YOUR NEW PRODUCT
Where should you begin to create your own pet product?
Start at home.

Create a prototype and try it out on your own pet. Watch
closely to see if it works. Does your dog like that new
recipe? Is the toy you envisioned actually holding up to
normal wear and tear? Does the new product entice your
cat as you hoped it would? If your product passes the
home test, start reaching out for other testers.

Try your new product out on pets belonging to friends and
family. Watch and document their reactions. Then find a
broader beta testing group. Ask for and listen to honest
feedback.

Be careful as you test your products on other people's pets.
Take every precaution since your product is still in its
development stage and may have safety issues that will
only become apparent as you beta test it.

Once you are confident that the product is good and safe,
and that the market is ready for it, begin to look at it in
terms of production.

- Record the recipe or the process. Put any unique
  formula in a safe place. Patent the product and
  process if you can; copyright anything you can.

Companies have been known to purchase safes and bank vaults to protect their work product. You can do the same.

- Confirm you can access all the raw materials reliably.

- Calculate the cost to make the product at scale. Include the cost of raw materials, labor, packaging, marketing, shipping and delivery, government compliance, legal fees, etc.; that is, all the things that go into calculating the actual cost of getting your product ready to be sold.

- Determine what the market will pay.

- Source consumer data to check your initial findings.

- Start to build your funnels to market.

Now is the time to get any and all governmental permits and approvals.

MANAGING YOUR BUSINESS
There's no need to rehash the basics of setting up a business, but manufacturing has unique needs beyond the creation of a new product or product line.

BUSINESS ENTITY AND LEGALITIES
As with all businesses, you need to create and maintain a business entity. Product production can be expensive and your legal and liability exposure can be great. Protect those investments and your personal assets by setting up a business entity that takes all that into account. An LLC may work for a dog walker; product production might need far greater legal protections. Speak with an attorney.

In anticipation of your sales, unless you are selling in your immediate area only, you will deal with taxes across jurisdictions. Each one has its own rates and regulations. Consult a tax expert to guide you through collecting and paying sales tax

In fact, unless you are a CPA or tax attorney, plan on hiring one. At the very least, have them on retainer. There are a lot of moving parts to a business such as this, even if all you do is get paid royalties for your creation by allowing a larger manufacturer to license your product.

The one caveat to needing professional tax support is if you intend to only sell your product online through a major e-commerce platform. These platforms are set up to deal with sales taxes for you.

INSURANCE
Before moving on to the nuts and bolts of setting up a product manufacturing business, insurance has got to be addressed. In short, get some!

In fact, you will probably need various types of insurance and as your business grows so will your insurance needs. Speak with a trusted expert who understands all your current and future risks and get the insurance they recommend.

MANUFACTURING FACILITY
The type of product you are creating and the market segment you are targeting will be large factors in determining what sort of facility you need for manufacturing.

If you are making handmade, one-of-a-kind leashes in your workshop and plan to sell them for several hundred dollars each (they're works of art, after all), you will likely never need a large manufacturing plant. You might need a larger workshop where you can hire a few assistants or few dozen artisans. Or you could remain a one-person show and never need space beyond a spare bedroom or garage. You may never need more than a small office space and a smartphone or tablet along with a few key business apps that can organize and track your entire supply chain as well as your sales funnels.

But producing hundreds of gallons a day of a new line of pet shampoos will require much more. You will need a manufacturing plant. You certainly do not need to build your own production line; at least not yet. But you do need to have access to a facility that meets your needs and standards and allows your business to grow.

Many manufacturing facilities have downtime and you could try to find one to rent during their off hours. If your product is food related, there are commercial kitchens available to rent, but not all of them will agree to having pet food cooked in them. Find one that will.

Alternatively you could turn to factories that are already set up to produce products like yours. These may manufacture products for your competitors but in reality, they are not owned by any brand; they simply contract out their facility, machines, and workforce to anyone willing to pay their fee. They are not looking to steal your ideas and they will not share your secrets (or shouldn't) with their other clients. They simply want to keep their production lines busy as that is their business model. If you are overly concerned with your idea getting stolen, distribute the risk by having different hubs (factories) produce individual components and manage the final production line where they all get put together. This is not particularly efficient but sometimes it is worth the added work and expense. In general though, it is better to simply find a reliable and trustworthy manufacturer.

When at some point you grow to the point where having your own factory is justified, you will be in a position to hire experts to guide you through design, building, and managing your own facility.

MARKETING AND YOUR SALES FORCE

While you are still starting out, your second biggest challenge and business expense, after the manufacturing process, will be marketing and sales. You could have the best product in the world but if people are unaware of it, how will potential customers know to buy it? Investing in sales pipelines, whether they are direct sales, online, or through third party retailers (more about these later), needs to start early and will continue for the life of your business. Invest heavily in these.

Establish procedures and protocols for your sales force; after all, they represent you. While your product may be unique, sales is sales. Look for existing employee manuals and modify them to suit your needs.

Finally, hire the best sales and marketing people you can. Pay them as well as you can. Incentivize them and perhaps more importantly, listen and learn from them.

BACK OF HOUSE PLATFORMS

In addition to your production line, your back of house needs the tools and staff that will control and track every aspect of the production, inventory, and sales. Invest in the proper software to track each aspect and if possible, find software that can integrate them all in one place.

Keep in mind that you cannot adequately oversee every aspect of your business for long; even with a slew of software. Plan to hire properly trained staff (or train them yourself) to whom you can delegate the day-to-day overseeing of your business':

- Finances
- Sales

Chapter 13.

- Logistics and supply chain
- Time management
- Staff

HOW AND WHERE WILL YOU SELL?
There are basically two avenues for sales: direct sales and through a third party (to whom you will sell wholesale).

DIRECT SALES
If you are able to reach your customers directly, you can eliminate the "middleman" and keep more of your profits. But that will require a dedicated sales force (human and digital) and a larger customer service department.

Direct sales require attending to any and all of the available avenues linking you and your customers.

1. Store-in-store or pop-up stores
   Supporting a brick-and-mortar store with one or two products is not realistic. But you may be able to team up with existing stores and create "shop-in-shop" opportunities. Essentially you will be subletting retail space. This gives you a brick-and-mortar presence without the brick-and-mortar commitment or overhead. You would be responsible for staffing and managing such a sales location. This business model has become more and more popular recently. You are tapping into the retailer's customers at virtually no expense from you other than rent.
2. Shows, expos, and events
   Attending community or industry shows is a very common way for new products and new entrepreneurs to reach the market. Booths are generally inexpensive. Attendees are there to support the businesses presenting their goods or to find great deals.

3. <u>Online</u>

For direct online sales, creating the right website and e-commerce store is crucial; in fact, it's everything. Hire professionals to build, or help you build, your online presence.

Even online you need a sales force. They may focus on social media campaigns or affiliate sales but they are still doing the selling and getting your products into customers' hands.

WHOLESALE

As a developer of a single product, your most likely avenue to market is to sell wholesale to larger retailers.

Your wholesale price needs to reflect their need to make a profit on top of yours. This usually means your income per item is less than what it might be if only you could have reached your customers directly. But since you can't (or you opt to reach your customers from multiple directions), look at the bright side of selling your products for a smaller profit: wholesale orders means selling a larger number of your products in a single sale. Since each sale costs you something, larger orders in fewer transactions may be actually more profitable.

To be considered by large retail outlets, you will need to prove that you have the production capacity in place to fulfill their orders before they commit to ordering from you. If your production is low or slow, avoid the larger stores and look to mom-and-pop pet supply stores. This will also give you an opportunity to work out any kinks in your production process before you go big.

THINKING OF FLYING SOLO?

Of all the pet industry businesses discussed so far, product manufacturing is by far the most complex with the greatest number of moving parts. Very few can do this alone. Get yourself a partner. Even if you love doing everything yourself, from product development to running the business, remember that there are only 24 hours in a day. You really cannot do it all; at least you cannot do it all well for very long. No one can. Find a partner, decide where each one's strengths lie, and let go. That does not mean you can ignore any part of your business. It means you share the burden while allowing each partner to oversee the area that best suits them and their skill set.

BITS AND PIECES FOR PRODUCT MANUFACTURERS

- Create products that add value and improve the lives of your customers. More of the same will get lost among the thousands of products that came before yours.

- Know and articulate who your target customers are.

- Protect your brand by ensuring your product delivers as promised.

- Protect your investment and your company by always being in compliance with regulatory requirements.

- Think big, start small, scale fast.

Chapter 14.
RETAIL PET SUPPLY BUSINESSES

Flexibility: Low (brick and mortar) to moderate (e-commerce)

Investment level: Moderate to very high

Startup costs: For an online (e-commerce) store an initial investment may be a few hundred dollars; for a brick-and-mortar store an initial investment will certainly be tens of thousands and upwards of hundreds of thousands of dollars

Mandatory education: None

Recommended education: Learn supply chain processes and software as well as the ins and outs of inventory tracking and logistics, bookkeeping and accounts reconciliation. For e-commerce: learn enough code to optimize and maintain your online store/website

Necessary equipment: For a brick-and-mortar store: retail space, standard business and retail store equipment such as shelves and display cases, cash register, credit card/phone scanners, UPC barcode scanners. For e-commerce: a computer; possibly warehouse space for inventory, barcode scanners, logistics software

Recommended equipment: Delivery van and shipping scales if you hold inventory; accounts with delivery services

Legal requirements: Establish a legal business entity; sales tax accounts; refunds and returns policies; business license (even for e-commerce); permit(s) to operate; insurance; payroll software/accounts, EIN

STARTING YOUR OWN RETAIL PET SUPPLY STORE

In the age of big box stores and mega e-commerce platforms, why would you consider starting a small retail outlet? Competing against established sellers might seem to be a fool's mission. How can a solitary, 'mom-and-pop' shop ever compete against them? These are legitimate concerns. But being small also has some advantages.

Most people prefer to shop where they trust, and people want to shop where their needs are met even if that means paying a little more. Of course, price and convenience are factors, but they are not the *only* factors.

You, as the owner of a small, local shop, have the ability to pivot quickly as trends change or as new products come into the market. You also have something that they do not have: your personal connection with your customers. They are likely your friends and neighbors.

Let's compare two shopping experiences.

Shopping experience number one: Customer A finds themselves in a large mega store offering thousands, if not tens of thousands, of products. The customer walks down aisle after aisle trying to find the product they are looking for. Even after finding the right section, they are now confronted with 5, 10, 15 competing products! Each differ slightly from one another. How can the customer be sure which is the better quality, which is the better buy, and which is better suited to their pet?

Compare that to *your* pet supply store where you are there to answer all their questions and to provide information on each carefully selected product. Over time you have the opportunity to really get to know their pets (and not just by relying on some mathematical algorithm that will suggest what they might buy next). You know what they like and what has worked in the past. And if you don't know, you are there, in real life, willing to find out.

Chapter 14.

As a small business owner, you have enormous flexibility when it comes to choosing your inventory. Big box stores may not risk precious shelf space for a new product, or one that targets a very small niche. But you can. In fact, you could build an entire business based on new and quirky products.

Even online, a small, well-curated e-commerce shop can be a more pleasurable and effective option for many customers. By offering either unique items or personalized service, you can compete.

To build a new retail business, you have 2 options. Purchasing an existing store (or franchise) or building one from scratch.

Buying an existing store or franchise has some advantages and some disadvantages. For instance, franchises tend to be heavily controlled and regulated by the franchise organization. You will have to do things their way and generally they decide what you can sell and for how much. Buying an established mom-and-pop store may seem like a great deal if they include their existing inventory, but you should question why that inventory is still hanging around. And why they are selling in the first place if the business is as successful as they claim. On the other hand, franchises have a large, experienced company supporting them and marketing may rest with the mothership. Existing mom-and-pop shops may come with a built-in loyal clientele.

Starting from scratch relieves you of the burden of endless compliance with a franchise; it eliminates the possibility of being associated with a possibly failed, or outdated, store. It gives you the freedom to create your business from the ground up. But it also places the burden of starting from zero completely on your shoulders.

Regardless of whether you are starting from scratch or buying an existing business, you first need to decide which type of retail store you want.

BRICK-AND-MORTAR OR E-COMMERCE?

<u>BRICK-AND-MORTAR</u>
The internet may have its sophisticated algorithms, but nothing beats a face-to-face conversation with someone who knows what their customers want. A key task of pet supply retailers is to be knowledgeable about the products they sell, the market, the trends, and the needs and wants of a diverse population of pet owners. Brick-and-mortar shoppers are looking for a personal experience. They are also looking for immediate gratification. They want to walk out with the product they came in for.

But, if you want to be successful, it is not enough to just stack bags of dog food or chicken feed and call it a day. Your customers will expect you to be able to direct them to the right product for their pets. They expect you to know what each product is made of and where it came from. While there is no need to denigrate any product you do not carry, your customers will want to know why product X, which you carry, is better than product Y, which they must buy elsewhere.

Owning a retail pet supply shop means anticipating needs and trends. Heavy winter blankets are not likely to sell well in July (unless you live in the southern hemisphere) and any product recently getting negative news coverage is going to sit in your inventory (and customers may question your integrity for not pulling it off the shelves). You need to stock, act, and react accordingly.

Brick-and-mortar stores tend to service their local community. Most consumers will not travel far to buy a product they can purchase close to home. That is, unless you give them a reason to come to your store.

If you offer home delivery for the convenience of your customers, you can expand your reach to a slightly larger region. Delivery can also be an attractive service to customers who live nearby but who can't lift heavy purchases such as large bags of pet food. Of course, even your very local business can ship anywhere. But the likelihood of a customer contacting you from across the country to order a product that they can get locally is very slim. However, if you carry items that are exclusive to you or are only available from a few outlets, you can create a loyal customer base from far and wide.

The main challenge to opening a brick-and-mortar retail outlet is that it requires a physical space for the shop, which can be an expensive commitment. It also means holding inventory of a lot of products, which again, is an expensive and risky commitment.

Having a brick-and-mortar pet supply store takes a lot of planning and constant research to anticipate needs and allow for shipping time from manufacturers and distributors. It might mean employing staff to keep the shop open enough hours a day to meet your goals. It means competing with "the big boys" that can always compete on price.

But the *added value* that local shops provide can help level the playing field.

E-COMMERCE

Despite the hype, despite what you might have heard, e-commerce businesses do not run themselves. It takes work to maintain your site, control your supply chain, and to market your store and the products you carry.

The internet is a busy, noisy place. Standing out and getting potential customers to your site is a challenge. Developing and maintaining relationships with customers is also a challenge. Competing with brick-and-mortar stores, where the customer leaves with their purchases in hand, is a challenge.

Yet, e-commerce has its advantages, too.

For the customer, an e-commerce store is always open. Some online stores employ international call centers to ensure that customers can connect with a human 24/7. Some e-commerce businesses use very sophisticated chatbots even if there is no human around.

For the business owner, there is a great deal of flexibility in owning an e-commerce store. You can work all night and sleep all day. You can work from home in your pajamas or from an internet café. You can work around family obligations. Your customers will never know.

A brick-and-mortar store is limited to sell only what they planned ahead for, ordered and received, and have in stock. Meanwhile, an online store can instantly add products while losing no time waiting for inventory to arrive. In fact, it is possible for e-commerce stores to never hold inventory at all, relying on drop shipping.

And, as trends and seasons change, you can change the look of your store, your prices, and your entire inventory - basically everything - with a few keystrokes.

A huge advantage e-commerce stores have is financial. They do not need a physical space and the monetary commitment which that requires. If your e-commerce store dropships, you need never invest in inventory. You will never have to get rid of last year's models, pet food will never expire on your shelves, and if a product sells very well, there is far less chance of you being "out of stock" unless the manufacturer itself has run out. Of course, if you *want* to control the entire supply line or ensure the availability of your products, you can hold inventory and ship out each order yourself from your central location.

Chapter 14.

MANAGING YOUR RETAIL BUSINESS

BUSINESS ENTITY
Regardless of format, all retail stores need to register as a business entity with the appropriate authorities. Even e-commerce businesses need to declare themselves to tax authorities.

Unless your brick-and-mortar store offers services that require bringing pets into your shop, such as grooming, you do not have to concern yourself with departments of health or agriculture, or local ordinances protecting animals; only those rules governing retail stores.

TAXES
All retail businesses doing business in jurisdictions with sales tax are required to collect (and then turn over) that tax. This means that you may need to set up tax accounts for every jurisdiction in which you sell. The advent of e-commerce has challenged tax authorities to determine who pays what, where, and how much since e-commerce sales cross state and even national borders. Plan to spend time dealing with sales tax authorities.

But do not let the bookkeeping put you off. Most, if not all, e-commerce host platforms are prepared for this and their software will walk you through the process. Your site will likely be pre-formatted to deal with sales tax across jurisdictions.

If you plan to sell remotely from your brick-and-mortar store, you should consult with a CPA who has experience in this area. It can be complicated.

Keep in mind that this topic is still evolving, and you should consult with tax experts regarding what your obligations are. You should regularly check for changes.

OTHER BOOKKEEPING

Recordkeeping is crucial for retail. You need to document each and every transaction. Fortunately, there are many mobile payment apps, credit card swipers, and software programs for this. These programs all provide accurate records of each transaction.

Your e-commerce host platform certainly provides this service to you. You will pay transaction fees, but the process is handled through the e-commerce host. Since cash payment is not an option electronically, all your e-commerce sales will be handled electronically.

In-store cash sales must be accurately recorded, not only for sales tax purposes, but for accurate income tax payments, and so that you can balance your books.

Other tax obligations are payroll taxes. Retailers with employees need to accurately record employee salaries and tax payments. As their employer, you will need to set up an account from which to pay their payroll taxes. Either invest in software to handle payroll or contract an outside payroll firm. Payroll may not be difficult, but it does need to be 100% accurate.

TECH FOR LOGISTICS

Besides payment apps and the typical devices all businesses need (phones, pc), you will need a cash register and credit card scanner. Another scanner you should invest in is a bar code or QR code scanner.

As each item comes into your store (virtually for e-commerce or in real life) you should assign it a code. You can choose to use the bar code it comes with, but if it doesn't have one already or if you want your inventory standardized, assign one of your own. This is for tracking inventory. There are many inexpensive scanner sets for you to choose from.

Chapter 14.

Retail locations and online shops holding inventory should consider investing in a system for attaching labels with QR codes, and not just bar codes, to each item. QR codes can contain a lot of details for each item that may prove to be useful and worth the investment.

Tracking with a computerized scanner system will help you to know precisely and continuously what you have in stock. Having all your stock accurately inventoried at all times will save you countless hours of work at tax time when inventory needs to be accounted for. It also makes ordering and restocking easier and more accurate.

BANKING
You will need at least one business bank account, but there is an argument to be made for opening more than one. Which ones?

- An account for employee taxes that your payroll is attached to

- Another account for sales taxes that can automatically turn over the sales tax you have created

- An account for your business' taxes

- And an account for in-store transactions into which purchases are paid and from which inventory is paid for

Cash transactions should be recorded immediately and deposited daily.

INSURANCE
The type and amount of insurance you will need for an e-commerce business differs from the insurance you need for a brick-and-mortar store.

- All retail businesses need to insure their inventory against damage or loss.

- Any employees must be insured against job-related injuries.

- Customers entering your brick-and-mortar store need to be covered in case of accident on your premises.

Speak with a qualified insurance broker who specializes in retail businesses.

PROTOCOLS AND PROCEDURES

There are two important documents you need to spend serious time thinking about and creating. They are an employee manual and a returns and refund policy.

An employee manual may not be necessary if you have no employees. But if you intend to have employees someday, start working on the manual sooner rather than later. Include all your policies and procedures. Include all protocols.

The second crucial document, your returns and exchange policy, can make all the difference in your bottom line. This is a legally binding agreement between you and your customers and is there to protect your business from people who could otherwise abuse your goodwill.

Many e-commerce host platforms have their own basic policy for returns. If theirs works for you, use it. If you are unhappy with any aspect of theirs, create your own and upload it to your webstore.

You could opt to download a generic returns and exchange policy, but paying an attorney to write one specific for you and your business may be the wiser route depending on the types of products you sell and whether you open a brick-and-mortar shop or e-commerce store.

Chapter 14.

LOCATION, LOCATION, LOCATION

They say location is everything when you buy a home. The same is true for situating your brick-and-mortar pet supply store.

Commit wisely to any location you rent or buy.

- Thoroughly research the zoning and what each location both offers and allows.
- Is there enough parking?
- What restrictions are there?
- Can you open and stay open when you want your shop to be open?
- Does it actually meet your needs (or come closest to meeting your needs) in terms of size and layout?
- Is it convenient for your customers?
- What are your legal obligations and what are the obligations your property owner has agreed to?

This may be your biggest investment for your business. It can make or break you. Choose and commit only after you do your due diligence.

Location is important for e-commerce sites, too. While virtual, your store is "located" based on SEO key words. Make sure your e-commerce store is easily located by wisely using the best SEO key words.

BRANDING

Once your entity is established and you have started to home in on the products you think you will sell, you can begin to brand your business.

Key to branding any store is knowing that no store can be all things to all people. No store can, nor should try to, carry everything for everyone. Equestrians do not expect to find saddles in their neighborhood pet supplier (unless you are in an equestrian-rich location); people with gerbils do not expect to find gerbil feed in a store catering to horses.

So, pick your niche and focus on that as you develop your brand.

ABCs OF BRANDING FOR RETAIL

You need to offer customers a reason to choose your store. Branding goes a long way to helping them choose.

What makes your retail store unique and stand out? And how can customers find you amidst all the noise your competitors are making? Answer those questions and you will have the core of your brand. Add that to your mission statement (from your business plan) and you can point clearly to your brand.

Besides offering products that no other retailer can secure, what might that be?

YOUR BUSINESS NAME

Finding a great name for your business is obviously important; it is also very hard to do in this sector. All the great names seem to have been taken already! But even if a name is already in use, it still might be available for you. If it hasn't been trademarked, it's available. If the name is in use in a different or distant market or region and you plan to stay local, there is no reason not to use it. Just make sure you are not the second or third "Puppy Palace" in town.

Be creative; but don't go overboard. In fact, being too cute can backfire. "Petz" with a "z" is overused and trite. It brings little or no added value.

For a local brick-and-mortar shop, consider what will speak to your customers living in your area. "Main Street Pet Supplies" is simple, to the point, and works if your store is on Main Street. "University Fur and Feathers" is

simple and relevant if your store is located near a
university. Do not overlook the practical, consider what
will fit on the sign. Literally.

For online stores, your domain, which is likely the same as
your store's name, is crucial because that is the only way
for your potential customers to find you. They can be
enticed, or be put off, by your name long before they see
your beautifully designed and curated online store. If your
business name is too long, people might mis-type it and
never find you. A name that is too cutesy (too many "z's"
in place of "s") or has a bizarre connotation that most
people do not immediately understand, might put off a lot
of potential buyers. Keep it simple.

Speaking of domains and protected names, before you
settle on a name for your store (in real life or for e-
commerce) do your homework and see if the dot-com
domain is available. The top level domain (TLD) ".com"
remains the gold standard. You can get by with a .net, but
at the present time, it is not as good.

MARKETING AND PR
As a new business, you will almost certainly not have the
resources your more established competitors have to spend
on marketing. You may never have the marketing budget
the big box stores have. But marketing, even in a highly
competitive environment, can be done, and done well, if
you are creative and know your target audience. It need
not cost millions. It just requires engagement.

Meet your potential customers where they are, offer them
solutions to their needs, and invite them in. Marketing
really is as simple as that.

Marketing, as has been stated before, is not selling. It is
not advertising, although advertising is a form of
marketing; so let's start there. Of all the pet industry

businesses examined so far, retail stores are the most likely to use traditional advertising effectively to increase business.

ADVERTISING

Creating engaging and effective ads is a skill that can be learned. Either learn to create your own or hire a professional. Some publications and mass media outlets have in-house teams that can help you.

If your store is high-end, advertise to, and engage with, groups able and willing to spend at your price point. There is no worth in spending resources (time or money) advertising to people who cannot afford your goods. Handing out coupons is not the way to attract this sector; hosting interesting, exclusive events in your store is. Offering exclusive content on your website or blog is, too. (see below)

At the other end of the spectrum, if your store is slated to sell lower cost items, there is no reason to advertise in media that attracts high-worth shoppers. The budget shopper is looking for deals. The budget shopper appreciates coupons.

You want to time your ad campaigns wisely in addition to targeting them well. Running a sale or promoting outdoor items for pets in the depths of a snowy winter will not win you customers and those products will not move, taking up precious shelf space. However, promoting outdoor pet supplies (for example: parasite preventives) just as Spring arrives, when parasites start to appear and people begin to plan their vacations, will be better timed and more effective.

Place your advertising in strategic publications. Social media may reach a lot of people and be great for an e-commerce store, but a community newspaper may be a better way to reach local shoppers.

Chapter 14.

BE ACTIVE AND ENGAGING ON SOCIAL MEDIA

You may not have the engaging photos a pet groomer has, but if you are creative you can develop a social media following with the content you *can* create.

- Post about what you know. Share information. Do not focus on selling but be sure to include subtle links to products which you sell that relate to whatever you are posting about.

- Be more than just a product source, be their pets' champion. Write about best practices for pet care.

- Write and share timely newsletters and announcements.

- Offer specials to repeat customers and offer more to your best ones.

- Create a cadre of loyal customers and followers to be your evangelicals who will review, like, and share all you do on social media.

CONNECT WITH LOCAL AND MASS MEDIA

Your local community newspaper and even your local TV news station want your advertising funds. But even if you do not have such funds, you *can* get media coverage.

If you host a local event in your store, let the local news know about it. All it takes is a well-written and enticing press release. If you are participating in an event, do the same. Do not assume the event's organizers have contacted the press. Even if they did, your business may not be on their radar. Put it there.

Offer to come on local morning shows to talk about various aspects of pet care and the products it takes to care for pets. Don't sell; inform. If they aren't interested in pet care, make yourself available as a local business owner and speak about running a business in your community.

For a wider reach, offer to be a guest on podcasts and syndicated shows.

<u>BE ACTIVE IN YOUR COMMUNITY</u>
Participate in and sponsor local events. Take a booth at local events as often as possible. Offer to speak to community groups about pet care.

Befriend, in a genuine way, complementary businesses such as local boarding kennels, vet practices, groomers, and other pet services providers. Offer these business owners discounts and refer your customers to them. Hopefully, in exchange, they will send their clients to you.

If you can, support your local pet organizations. Rescues can always use donated goods. If you cannot afford to donate goods, you can donate your time or your space. Periodically let local rescues set up a table in your store to drum up support for their causes. Online, place links to a few rescues on your website. It costs you nothing.

Hopefully your store will keep you busy and you will achieve all your financial goals through it. If it does not, or it does not get you there fast enough, there are ways to leverage your store for expanding your revenue streams. Even if your store is a resounding success, you may want to consider adding supplementary revenue streams within your retail setting. These may not only contribute to your bottom line, your customers may appreciate them, too.

EXPAND YOUR REVENUE STREAMS FOR BRICK AND MORTAR STORES
1.Offer additional services
Additional services work two ways. It brings in new retail customers who show up for that service, while retail customers are potential clients for the add-on. Additional services you might consider are grooming or small pet

daycare, but only if you have the space, the infrastructure, and the proper zoning.

2. After-hours use of your facility
Your store may be open from 9 to 5, but you are paying rent or a mortgage for it 24/7. Maximize the use of that space.

If your store is large enough, why not host after-hours classes? These could be anything from Pet CPR classes to obedience training for dogs (if you have enough space for that). If your store has an outdoor element, you could hold classes outside even during your regular hours of operation since they will not interfere with sales inside.

Hire instructors, or partner with instructors and split the income.

3. Add an e-commerce option
You can build an online store that completely meshes with your brick-and-mortar. Instead of coming into the shop, your customers can place their orders – or recurring orders - online and have them delivered. By offering same day delivery you can compete with other online shops that may take days or weeks to deliver.

Alternatively, you could maintain a pet-product e-commerce store under a completely different name, a different brand, and one which has nothing to do with your current brick-and-mortar store.

Just keep in mind that e-commerce stores do not run themselves, they require your attention and take time to manage.

4. Add locations or franchise
Once your first store is successful, you may want to branch out and open a second location. There is virtually no end to the number of stores you can own. Each store gets easier as you gain more experience. The cost of your back

of house services can be shared by several locations and your buying power for wholesale purchases increases as your inventory orders grow.

Owning and overseeing multiple stores can be challenging. You will need to hire store managers, more employees, pay more rent. But this is how all large chain stores started. If they can do it, so can you.

Alternatively, once you have a proven success, you could expand your business by selling franchises. As noted earlier in this book, franchising is a complex (albeit completely do-able) business model for which the first step would be to speak with an experienced and dependable franchise attorney.

SECONDARY INCOME STREAMS FOR ONLINE RETAIL STORE OWNERS

1. Additional e-commerce sites

In theory, there are no limits to the number of e-commerce sites you could maintain. Each one can expand your reach. Consider a second site for products that do not meet the mission or market of your initial e-commerce store. If your first online shop caters to only high-end domestic pet parents, open an e-commerce store to serve a niche pet sport. Or focus on particular breeds or different species. The sky is the limit.

2. Write a pay-walled blog or create content for a fee. Since you will be online anyway, why not create pet-related or pet industry-related content for sale? It may take time but if you create interesting, dynamic content and build a following, people will pay to view it. You could even offer your content creation services to other pet industry businesses.

Write a blog if you like to write; create video content if you prefer that medium.

3. Affiliate sales

There are companies that will pay you to promote their products. They will provide you a code that you can share with your followers. For each purchase made using that code you will receive a small fee. Professional bloggers do this all the time; you can too. You do not need to restrict yourself to only those products you sell.

BITS AND PIECES FOR PET INDUSTRY RETAIL BUSINESSES

- Be clear about your legal obligation regarding products. Consult an attorney when drafting your product liability policy as well as your return and exchange policy.

- Stay informed about trends and new products. Get to know your clientele and always be looking for ways to address their needs.

- Work with your fellow pet care professionals in your area and see what they need and what products they want their clients to buy and then stock those.

- Having endlessly diverse products in your store can be overwhelming and may not increase sales. Stick to your brand.

- Build community. Freely share information about products and care with your customers and do the same with your fellow professionals.

Chapter 15.
STARTING A DOGGY-DAYCARE

Flexibility: Very low to moderate

Investment level: Moderate to very high

Startup costs: From as little as a few hundred dollars to hundreds of thousands of dollars

Mandatory education: None

Recommended education: business management, bookkeeping, K9 CPR, dog behavior and psychology, basic dog training

Necessary equipment: Besides a suitable -and legal-location, you will need runs or crates, a supply of leads, a few muzzles, a first aid kit for both humans and dogs, water dishes, towels

Recommended equipment: Basic grooming supplies, pest treatments and preventatives, van or vehicle for pickups and drop offs, toys, play equipment

Legal requirements: Business entity registration, business license, certificates from all appropriate governmental health departments and animal control, business bank account, taxpayer ID and account with the tax authorities, insurance

WHAT IS DOGGY DAYCARE AND WHO NEEDS IT?
In theory it's possible to offer daycare for any type of animal, but without a doubt, the most common is daycare for dogs.

Doggy daycare is a hybrid between pet sitting and a boarding kennel. It offers a bit of each but differs significantly from both.

This is not an overnight boarding facility, though some boarding kennels do offer daycare services and some daycares offer overnight boarding. You are in fact dog sitting; but not in their home and this is a group setting.

The most common reason people utilize doggy daycare is because they provide a safe, engaging environment for dogs during the day instead of having to leave a dog at home alone with no one to care for them. Staying home alone provides minimal stimulation and exercise. Some pet parents who work from home also choose to send their dog to daycare because even though they are at home, they cannot provide *enough* attention, care, or stimulation for their dogs.

A second common reason dogs come to daycare is to develop or improve their dog-to-dog socialization skills. During their time at daycare, dogs are permitted, and even encouraged, to interact with other dogs who are also there for the day.

Some dogs come to daycare several times a week; others come a little less often. Occasionally there are dogs who join in every day. Usually daycares mandate minimal participation. To the outsider that might look like the operators wanting to maximize their income. In fact, it's to ensure that the pack gets to know each member and no dog needs to reacclimate each visit.

Do not be fooled by what looks like happy mayhem in the doggy daycares you may have visited. Well-run daycares are very structured and coordinated. This is to protect all the dogs in their care at all times. It is also to protect the workers.

A DAY IN THE LIFE OF DOGGY DAYCARE
A typical day in daycare might look something like this:

- Open facility from 6am to 7am (prep waters, last minute set-ups, return phone calls/emails, check intake list and payments)
- Intake of dogs from 7am to 8am (check in dogs, accept payments, check immunizations, etc.)
- Free play until 9:00
- Organized activities from 9am to noon
- Siesta and quiet time from noon to 3pm (some staff in the office taking care of business; others cleaning, prepping, caring for dogs)
- All dogs out to relieve themselves from 3pm to 4pm
- Free play until pickup between 4pm and close
- Clean facility (indoors, yard, laundry, etc.)
- Prep for the next day

It's a busy day and it takes a team. There are a lot of moving parts. A lot can happen in an instant, and things can go downhill quickly.

There are unique risks associated with caring for multiple dogs, especially when you combine dogs from a host of different backgrounds, each who have had various levels of training.

Dogs are pack animals and pack mentality can override training under certain circumstances, turning normally well-behaved dogs into a mob. In fact, even the best-behaved dogs can be pushed beyond their limits and will lash out under stressful conditions. Daycare can be stressful. Injuries occur, accidents happen.

These conflicts and disruptions can be exacerbated if attendants are not well trained or are not paying enough attention. It's up to staff to control each and every dog while allowing the group to have fun.

Aside from keeping each dog safe and under control, your clients expect you to keep their dog healthy. Bringing multiple dogs together can result in outbreaks of illness or infestation of parasites. It's up to you to set and enforce a level of cleanliness to protect each dog in your care.

The best way, perhaps the only way, to mitigate these risks is for everyone on your team to be well trained and on the same page. The only way to achieve those goals is to have in place well-developed procedures and protocols aimed at protecting everyone and everything at the doggy daycare facility.

PROTOCOLS AND PROCEDURES
Before you begin to create protocols and procedures for your business, try to speak with other doggy daycare providers and ask about theirs. Ask to see their employee manual. If they do not have one, find out what their employee training is like and what, in their opinion, are the most important things their employees do, or should do. Then sort through all of their suggestions and start to develop your own manual.

It won't be until you open that you will know what actually works best for you and what you might have initially overlooked. Procedures, protocols, and employee manuals are not set in stone. You will most likely revise and add to them as you learn. That's fine, but start somewhere and have some basic rules, guidelines, and policies in place before you open your doors to clients.

Even if your business is humming along smoothly, it is a good idea to review your policies, procedures, and protocols on a regular basis and then review them with your employees.

Chapter 15.

MINIMUM MANDATORY REQUIREMENTS FOR HEALTH AND SAFETY

Safety begins at registration. Begin by creating those protocols that address your requirements before any dog can be considered for your facility.

Create a thorough and detailed registration form and evaluation process that provide an in-depth picture of who the dog is and what its strengths and weaknesses are in terms of getting along in the somewhat stressful situation of daycare. This should include the following:

PROOF OF IMMUNIZATION

Dogs in daycare should be immunized. This is to protect themselves as well as the other dogs in your care. Check with your local authorities for which immunizations are required by law and then check with a local vet or animal control to check which vaccines are recommended in your area. Insist on documentation (proof of immunization) from a reliable vet clinic. Keep each dog's record up to date. Do not make exemptions.

NOTE: In case you personally take issue with vaccinations, doggy daycare might not be for you. Most municipalities and health departments require all dogs to be vaccinated to some degree. Almost all require businesses caring for dogs to mandate compliance for each guest. If you are found to have allowed unvaccinated dogs into your facility, not only would some clients leave you, the authorities may fine you or even shut your business down.

HEALTH CERTIFICATES

Consider requiring an overall and up-to-date health certificate issued by the dog's vet. This is different from a record of immunization. This can protect you from claims by unhappy clients. If a dog has a pre-existing condition you are not able to accommodate, you need to know.

<u>PARASITE CONTROL AND TREATMENTS</u>
Fleas, ticks, and intestinal worms can infest your entire facility from a single carrier. Making preventative treatment mandatory is the only way to mitigate the risk. Consider getting approval to treat dogs if they are found to be infested. Otherwise, put into place a policy that dogs found to be infested must be immediately retrieved and taken home and can only return with proof of successful treatment.

<u>EVALUATION</u>
All dogs should be evaluated before being accepted as a daycare client. The evaluation is to see how the dog interacts and connects with staff and dogs.

A proper evaluation should begin with introducing the candidate to a single dog who is proven to be friendly, confident, and stable. If the candidate does well, bring in another dog, then another. Eventually try a dog who, while friendly and well behaved, emits a much more boisterous energy. If the candidate does well with all those, this is probably a dog that will do well in daycare.

Once a dog has been evaluated and accepted into daycare, they should be on probation for a time to ensure they are a good match for the rest of the dogs on site.

Only experienced evaluators should be the ones doing this evaluation and it must be in a controlled environment for the safety of all the dogs involved.

NOTE: Not all dogs are suited for all daycare situations. Refer on any dogs you cannot safely add to your mix.

CREATE RULES GOVERNING ENTRY AND EXITS OF DOGS
The two riskiest points for a dog in daycare can be at their entry to, and departure from, your facility.

When two dogs, each excited to see their owners at the end of the day (or excited to seeing their daycare buddies upon arrival), cross paths in a small lobby, their heightened excitement can trigger a confrontation. Do all you can to minimize and control that encounter or eliminate it completely.

Additionally, entry and exit times are when dogs are the most at risk for slipping away if not completely under the control of your staff or their owner. To protect against accidental escape, your facility should be designed with multiple levels of security barriers as well as protocols governing drop off and pick up.

ENTRY PROTOCOLS

To help ensure that no two dogs can get into a confrontation, or that any dog gets loose, all dogs need to be on a leash when not within the confines of the daycare room or yard. This leash rule should apply to the parking lot as well. Make sure your clients understand this rule and that it is for their safety, their dog's safety, and that it is non-negotiable. Habitual non-compliance should result in dismissal from daycare. For those clients who forget their dog's leash, have a few slip leads on hand.

Have your clients leave their dog's leash with you for use at pick up at the end of the day so there is no risk of them "forgetting" it in their car.

Drop-off may be a very hectic time with many dogs checking in at once while their human may be rushing to work and distracted. Be thorough anyway.

Before checking a dog in, give them a quick once-over to see if they appear healthy and without issues. Have a quick word with their human to make sure there have been no signs of illness or injury at home.

Get from your client any information that is lacking or outdated in their dog's records. This is something that should be red-flagged by your facility management software. You'll see it when you click on that dog's records to check him or her in.

Take one dog at a time into the playroom or play yard. Make sure your staff attendant is aware of each dog as they enter. Have a protocol for confirming each entry with staff. Keep tabs on your numbers.

<u>EXIT PROTOCOLS</u>
At the end of a busy day in daycare, most dogs are tired. Your staff is tired, too, and pet-parents may be in a hurry. Don't let any of that interfere with your exit protocols and procedures.

Do all you can to prevent conflicts at check-out. Complete the check-out process (payment) before bringing the client's dog out. Even if it means clients waiting a few minutes, handle one dog at a time only. Behind the scenes your staff can be readying the next few dogs.

Before handing over any dog, be 100% sure that the right dog is going home with the right family. If you think mistakes aren't made and the wrong dog never goes home with the wrong family, think again. Imagine a situation where owners are in a hurry to pick up their dog. Staff is dealing with 20 or 25 dogs all needing to be picked up within a short window. You have 3 or 4 adult Golden Retrievers who spent the day with you. They are all male. They are all approximately the same size. More than one of them is called Buddy. Can you see how things might get confusing? Have proper protocols in place so the right dog goes home with the right family and that no one gets left behind.

Check IDs. Be 100% sure that only those authorized to pick up a dog have access to them. If you are not sure, call the owners. Document the entire exchange.

Chapter 15.

Count your dogs. You and your staff should be counting dogs all day. This is particularly important at the end of the day to ensure all dogs are picked up and accounted for.

Close out your reservations and books each evening. This, too, will ensure all dogs were accounted for and have gone home.

EMERGENCY SITUATIONS
While we all hope never to have to deal with dozens of dogs during an emergency, it happens. The best way to mitigate stress, panic, or a bad outcome is to have a plan in place and to regularly rehearse that plan with your staff.

There are basically three types of emergencies you need to plan for and practice reacting to:

- Natural catastrophe emergencies
- Fire
- Outbreak of illness or an injury

With all the modern tracking and warning systems, it is rare that natural catastrophes happen without notice, except perhaps earthquakes. It is up to you to follow weather reports and be prepared. Sometimes the best course of action is to close your facility and not have any dogs in your care until the danger has passed, as in the case of foreseeable blizzards or typhoons.

But in the event that you just might find yourself facing a disaster with dogs on site, have a plan. Have a plan for keeping them safe and have a plan for getting them returned to their families.

Your plan should consider the following:

- You may not have time to put on collars and attach leashes. Have at least one slip lead for each dog. Place these leashes in strategic places around your

267

facility. Have attendants carry or wear a few leads at all times.

- Where can you safely hold the dogs in your care. Have a clear plan for getting dogs tethered and then taken to the furthest point in your fenced yard.

- Assign one team member to be responsible for contacting clients. This person should carry a phone with all the relevant phone numbers at all times.

These are only a few basic suggestions and examples. Construct your own procedures based on your facility and the number of dogs you care for each day. Then practice! Just as we practiced fire drills in school, you need to practice your emergency responses.

Outbreaks of illness can start anywhere and at any time. A dog that looked great at check-in could show signs of illness by noon. A dog that was fine all day could develop symptoms after they return home.

Your reaction will depend on what the illness is.

If the problem is discovered during the dog's stay and not after hours, your protocols should address when and how to isolate that dog. You should also have rules in place for getting that dog picked up immediately and procedures for cleaning and sterilizing your facility.

If that particular illness or condition requires treating your entire play yard (some diseases transmit through feces), it will mean that your entire yard needs to be treated before any dog is allowed out into it. If it is an airborne disease, your A/C duct system may need sterilizing. You may have to close down for a day or more to treat the problem. Have protocols in place that address these types of scenarios.

Chapter 15.

Do not forget that part of these protocols should include informing all your clients of the situation, not just the owner of the sick dog.

Fights: While not an emergency, Fights need to be anticipated. Avoiding clashes is the best defense against a fight breaking out. But realistically, chances are good that sooner or later a fight will break out in your daycare. How you and your staff react will make all the difference in how it will impact your business and the dogs in your care. Make sure your staff knows how to break up a fight quickly and safely. Restore order to all the dogs. Examine all the dogs involved for injuries and either treat or seek professional treatment. Immediately report the incident to the owners of any dog involved. At pickup, report the incident to all the other owners. You could even follow up that day with a group text or email explaining what occurred (do not bad-mouth any particular dog or even name the dog or dogs who started it). Let everyone know how this will be prevented in the future. Take time to review with your staff what happened and what everyone needs to learn from the experience.

A FEW MORE NOTES ABOUT SAFETY PROTOCOLS
Once dogs are in your facility it is on you to control the pack.

- Do not take on more dogs than you and your staff can safely manage. Set a maximum limit and stick to it.

- The size of your facility and yard should be more than adequate for the number of dogs each day.

- Maintain a good staff to dog ratio.

- Keep the dogs active and engaged (a tired dog is a good dog).

- Choose activities wisely, based on your numbers, the types and sizes of dogs in your care, and the experience of your staff.

- Give every dog a chance, but if a dog cannot integrate and is a danger to others, let the pet parent know this is not a good fit for them. Have procedures that protect you legally, for the possibility of having to dismiss a client.

PLANNING AND DESIGNING YOUR FACILITY
Doggy daycares come in all shapes and sizes. You should have access to a safe and secure outdoor space, in addition to your indoor playroom. Weather typically dictates how much time dogs can spend outside and your facility should reflect that.

If you live in a sunny, dry climate, the dogs in your care can spend a large portion of the day outside. You might need to ensure shade in your yard, but your indoor space might need to be smaller than a daycare located where it rains a lot or snows all winter.

Cold weather doggy daycares might opt for in-floor heating; investing in a heating system for your driveway may not be the luxury it initially sounds like, if it saves you the time or money daily snow removal would cost.

Some daycares separate larger dogs from the little ones; each group getting their own room and outdoor space. Some daycares separate dogs based on age. Other daycares divide the pack into smaller groups and rotate each small group among the activities. Whatever works for you is best as long as safety remains your top priority. Either plan your facility to suit your business model or plan your business model to suit your facility.

Whether you design it yourself or hire a professional, when planning, building, and outfitting your day care facility, KISS: Keep It Super Simple and… Keep It Simple & Smart.

In planning you need to consider:

- Flooring options
- Ceiling options
- Insulation for noise and temperature
- Rooms and their uses
- Types of enclosures (if any)
- Water sources
- Placement of electrical points
- Storage space
- Outdoor areas
- Security and security systems
- Bathrooms
- ADA compliance
- Lobby and reception (to suit logistics and protocols)
- Parking

Since safety is the primary concern, install appropriate fencing and design your facility to have multiple layers of barriers to prevent dogs from escaping. A single door between a dog and a busy road will sooner or later end badly. Installing multiple doors and gates may not eliminate *all* risks, but they will mitigate them. Redundancy in this area is a good thing.

Invest in equipment and activities to keep dogs engaged and not bored. Invest in good quality play yard equipment and toys so you do not have to replace them often. Be sure to have enough distractions for all the dogs; dogs experience jealousy and this can lead to fights.

If you intend to separate dogs according to size and have a "large dog" room and a "small dog" room, equip them appropriately.

If dogs will be crated during "quiet time" or fed while in your care, invest in the best crates you can afford. The same goes for dog beds and mats. Make sure your crates are the appropriate size for each dog. Too big is fine, too small is not.

Stock up on slip leads. Have on hand a few muzzles (just in case), plenty of towels, a few brushes, and a well-stocked first aid kit (for both staff and dogs).

Have plenty of water dishes, place them strategically throughout your facility including the play yard, and keep them filled. Be aware though, not all dogs know how to swim and it doesn't take deep water for a puppy or disoriented senior to drown.

Your facility will need reception space which can, if need be, double as an office. It is here that dogs will be checked in and checked out, payments will be made, and all non-dog-care related activities (such as returning calls and booking future dogs) will take place. This does not have to be elaborate, but it must be well-thought out. Build a barrier to protect your desk from jumping dogs and nosy clients wanting to see your computer screen.

Set up a monitoring system. While dogs should never be unattended, this monitoring system is for you to have extra eyes on everything all the time. This does not have to be an expensive, high-tech system with lots of bells and whistles. There are reasonably priced monitoring systems that will do the job just fine and will allow you to monitor your entire facility from your office.

Try to set aside a breakroom for your staff.

Chapter 15.

BUSINESS NEEDS

The businesses in the previous chapters all began by establishing a business entity. You will need to do the same for your daycare. But even before you establish a legal business entity, you should check your local ordinances regarding the care of animals in the jurisdiction where you hope to set up your business. Be sure you are allowed to run a doggy daycare in the first place!

Once you are sure you are allowed to open a doggy daycare where you want, be sure you are permitted to open this business in the specific facility you intend to buy or rent because zoning may be another obstacle to your plans. Once you are in the clear, you can get busy setting up your business.

BUSINESS ENTITY

Establish a legal business entity based on your specific needs and in consultation with a CPA or attorney.

Even though doggy daycare is far more complex than pet sitting, surprisingly, you may be able to safely work within a simple LLC framework no different than a one-person pet sitting business might.

Next, find the right bank to work with.

BANKING AND FINANCIALS

Like all businesses, you will need at least one business bank account. While at your bank, open as many different business accounts as necessary (one for payments, one for taxes, another for payroll, etc.).

Set up all the related financial accounts you will need such as mobile payment apps and accounts with credit card processing companies.

Set up payroll software or hire a third party to handle your payroll. Invest in software that tracks your employees' hours. Find a reliable CPA to at least audit your books, if not oversee all your taxes.

If in your jurisdiction you need to collect sales tax for services, set up that account with the tax authorities.

TECH HARDWARE AND SOFTWARE

You will need, at a minimum, a top-tier smartphone or tablet; but you may want to manage your doggy daycare on a desktop or laptop computer.

Invest in the best daycare scheduling software you can afford after researching all your options and finding the ones that work best for you. There are many on the market. Consider only those with good tech support.

INSURANCE

Acquire as much of the best insurance possible. This is a high-risk business, and you need to protect yourself, your staff, the dogs in your care, and visitors to your facility.

LEGAL DOCUMENTS

It is imperative that you have a contract that not only clearly states what services and care you provide, but also clearly explains what your clients' obligations are. It is highly recommended that an attorney experienced in this area prepare this document.

ADDITIONAL REVENUE STREAMS

Whether or not your daycare is reaching your financial goals, you may be interested in additional revenue streams. Here are a few suggestions that work well with daycares you might consider.

DOG TRAINING

You could offer training classes after hours. These could include classes in obedience, agility, rally, or several other sports, depending on the size of your facility. You would not necessarily even have to be there if you either hire instructors or rent out your space to a third party.

Chapter 15.

<u>TEACH</u>
Offer classes for pet owners such as pet-CPR or other pet-related topics. These can be scheduled for after the daycare closes for the evening or on the weekends (when most doggy daycares are closed) and might only require the purchase of additional chairs for your students. Either get certified to teach the curriculum or hire a third-party instructor. You could either pay them outright or split the registration fees.

<u>OFFER DAYCARE DURING NON-TYPICAL HOURS</u>
Dog owners will pay a premium to have their pets cared for when they themselves work less traditional hours. If you are located near a large hospital or a 24/7 manufacturing hub, you might find a very receptive niche market in the late or overnight shifts. You may need additional staff to cover these hours, but the payoff could be worth the added expense.

<u>RETAIL</u>
Add a pet supply component to your business. If your reception area is large enough, display your products. Even without a fully stocked retail corner, you can set up a small display and catalog and provide your clients with the opportunity to purchase good quality products that you have curated for them.

Of course, adding an e-commerce store under your daycare's banner is always an option and is something that does not need to interfere with the running of your core business.

BITS AND PIECES FOR DOGGY DAYCARE BUSINESSES
- Never over-extend and take on more dogs than you can safely care for. Accepting too many dogs is a recipe for disaster.

- Never let a sick dog into your daycare facility. Likewise, never knowingly let a dog with parasites in.

- Consider not accepting female dogs in season (in heat) into your facility. Even if every other client is a female, this can lead to fights. Male dogs coming in, even days later, can become agitated.

- Never let your staff bring food into the dog room or dog yard. Do not offer treats to your guests. Both can trigger fights.

- Do not play favorites unless you want to instigate fights. Dogs get jealous too.

- Make sure your staff is well trained. Even experienced staff from other facilities should be trained in the way you want your daycare run. Always supervise less experienced staff.

- If you feel you must offer a water component, such as a pool or pond, take extra caution. Not all dogs swim or swim well, and dogs can drown in very shallow water (not unlike small children).

Chapter 16.
BUILDING A BETTER BOARDING KENNEL

Flexibility: Extremely little to none

Investment level: Moderate to very high

Startup costs: From as little as a few hundred dollars to hundreds of thousands of dollars or more

Mandatory education: None

Recommended education: Business management, bookkeeping, animal husbandry (knowledge and extensive experience caring for whatever types of animals you will accept for boarding)

Necessary equipment: Can range from none to a few crates all the way up to a fully equipped boarding facility; various sized leads; water and food dishes; toys; complete first aid kit (for humans and pets)

Recommended equipment: All of the above plus: a bathtub, designated grooming area, quarantine area, basic OTC medications; treats; food.

Legal requirements: Proper zoning; establishment of a business entity, business license, certificates from appropriate government health or product safety departments, certificates to operate, insurance

WHY BUILD A BOARDING BUSINESS?
Do you remember when, at the beginning of this book, you were warned not to get into this industry if all you want to do is play with kittens and puppies? Well, no segment of this industry illustrates this rule better than boarding kennels.

Running a boarding kennel encompasses facets of every other business in the pet industry. As the boarding provider, you are the pet sitter and dog walker (dogs are the majority of boarding guests). You need to be educated about pet nutrition, pet foods, and pet products and you should be familiar with their manufacturing process and ingredients. You may even be called on to "manufacture" some meals, or other pet products, of your own. Some kennels offer pickup and delivery services and some offer transportation coordination for pets traveling for relocation. There are kennels that offer the services of a groomer, but even those that do not have a professional groomer on staff may offer a pre-pickup bath or a brush-out. Kennels may have a small retail store and some have been known to provide their clients photos of their pets having a great time while boarding. It's a lot. A lot, a lot.

Pet boarding is 24/7. Even when you are not physically seeing to your guests' needs, you are worrying about the animals in your care. "Stuff" happens and when owners cannot be reached, it is the kennel owner who makes the decisions, sometimes life and death decisions, on behalf of their customers and more importantly, on behalf of the animals entrusted to them.

Kennels are complicated with lots of moving parts. They are hard on you physically, mentally, and emotionally. There are endless opportunities for serious complications and even catastrophe.

In addition to caring for your guests, you will need to step up and be the resident troubleshooter for malfunctioning doggy doors, misfiring software, backed up toilets, and pets suffering from "stress diarrhea".

Why would you do this to yourself??

Chapter 16.

Because, in exchange for all that work and all that risk, when done well, boarding kennels can be extremely profitable.

Boarding kennels make good business sense. When money is tight, pet owners cut back where they can. They can cut back or eliminate daycare or the dog walker. They can have their pets groomed less often. They can cut back on the number of toys, accessories, or treats they buy or they may downgrade their pet's food.

But when they need to travel out of town or need to get their dog out of the house overnight for some other reason, dog owners have *no choice* but to find someone to care for their dogs.

In theory, could they ask a neighbor? Yes. But it only takes one bad experience and they will never again leave their pets with anyone other than a professional. The neighbor's home is probably not set up to prevent accidental escape. The neighbor might not know pet-CPR. If there is another dog in the house, how will this neighbor keep everyone safe? No, a neighbor is not the solution. Professional boarding is.

Yet, despite a vast and ever-growing need and a pet industry that seems unstoppable, boarding kennels fail regularly; others limp along, earning a living but just barely.

Didn't you just read that boarding kennels can be extremely profitable and sustainable? It's true. But far too few are. Few are successful enough to be sold at a profit unless the deal includes real estate, which ends up being the bulk of the kennel's worth. Why? Because owners didn't do their homework and they didn't plan appropriately. They didn't treat their pet care business as a business.

On top of all your other roles, for your kennel to succeed you must also be an educated and engaged business owner.

You must have a clear vision, backed up with data, and you need to prepare and be prepared. You need to prepare your facility, train quality staff, and create and enforce your protocols. You must have a grasp on the industry and your target market. Second only to the health and safety of your guests, your financials will drive every decision you make. You must know, really know, where you are financially, where you want to go, and how you are going to get (and stay) there.

Armed with the right research, good management skills, and high standards, you can create a business that is sustainable, profitable, and whose worth resides in the business, not the land it sits on. And who knows? You may never want to sell your kennel, instead, keeping it as a business that gets handed down generation to generation.

You might even get to play with puppies or kittens on occasion.

DIFFERENT BOARDING KENNEL MODELS
To board a pet means leaving a pet overnight with a caregiver away from home. Most kennels offer boarding for dogs or cats; the dog boarding market surpasses cat boarding manyfold. Some kennels accept both. Far less common are kennels that will also care for small house pets such as hamsters, gerbils, lizards, or birds, but they do exist (this is a great niche market to consider).

On the large animal side, horse boarding stables are, at their core, similar to dog boarding kennels. Horse owners expect the facility to be clean and safe, and for their horses to receive the best care possible. But, unlike dog or cat owners who only board their pets sporadically, horse owners often board their horse year-round when they themselves do not have adequate space or their own facilities. These are long-term commitments, and the owner may be much more involved in the day-to-day care of their pet. For the reader interested in horse boarding, this chapter has information relevant to you, too, even if it is geared primarily toward dog-boarding.

The reasons a domestic pet might need boarding varies. It could be the owner is on a business trip or vacation. A family renovating a house might not want their dog underfoot nor want to risk their cat getting out through a door accidentally left open. Some pets are boarded during fireworks seasons to better protect them and lessen any risk of them running away in fear. Occasionally a pet rescue will find themselves having to board a rescue animal as the last resort (due to their limited operating budget), rather than leave the pet in a bad situation.

Building a boarding facility to answer the needs of those pets can take many different forms. There are several models of boarding kennels for you to choose from, depending on your goals and resources.

IN-HOME BOARDING
Some boarding business owners choose to have their business in their home. This in-home model has both upsides and downsides.

The number of dogs that can stay in this "facility" is usually limited. Even in the largest home, having too many dogs roaming freely inside, especially dogs that typically do not live together, can be a challenge. It can even be risky. Unrestricted contact between dogs can result in fights breaking out in a heartbeat. And being left unrestricted to roam the boarding-house could lead to dogs causing damage or getting hurt.

Zoning or HOA restrictions may also restrict the number of dogs allowed at one time on a given property. This may make an in-home boarding business difficult to scale to profitability or unsustainable.

On the other hand, there is no additional rent or mortgage to pay on a facility if you board dogs in your home. You, as the business owner, would have no commute and could carry on with your daily life for the most part.

An in-home boarding arrangement usually allows the guest-dogs to have free run of the home alongside the owner's dogs and other guests. This can be a good situation for a dog that gets along with most other dogs, is one who is not likely to try to run away, and who may have had a bad experience in a traditional kennel. But not all dogs can adapt to this situation, particularly dogs that do not have a suitable temperament and do not "play well with others". This limits the reservoir of dogs available to the business owner to draw from.

The biggest risk for this type of boarding is that there *is* a relatively high chance of a guest escaping, as most homes do not provide multiple barriers and safeguards to ensure that a dog does not get out.

In-home boarding typically does not charge as much as a freestanding facility, but since the overhead is less, the bottom line might be attractive to you.

TRADITIONAL BOARDING KENNELS
Traditional boarding kennels have enclosures (runs) where individual dogs (or cats) stay. Dogs are typically taken out to a yard to play and get exercise daily or several times a day. There may or may not be interaction between unrelated guests at these set playtimes. Many, perhaps most, traditional boarding kennels prevent all interaction between guests. Even facilities that do allow their guests to play together, traditional boarding kennels house their guests separately. During meals, quiet time, and at night, dogs are segregated into own runs or crates.

282

Chapter 16.

To the outsider, dog runs may look like jail or an animal shelter. To the educated eye, this is the safest scenario for most pets. There is less concern about animals fighting and there are multiple barriers to prevent escape. All activities can be controlled. And the risk of cross-contamination from disease or parasites is lessened greatly, even if they cannot be eliminated completely.

This is typically the priciest of all kennel facilities to set up. The cost to maintain a traditional facility is also high. Typically there is rent or a mortgage to pay. Unless you buy an established kennel, you will spend time and money (and many sleepless nights) designing, building, and outfitting this new facility. Most kennels need some staff; some large boarding facilities need a lot of staff. There is the physical facility and a lot of equipment to maintain.

The payoff of all that investment is that the ROI can be the highest of all the boarding business models. The traditional kennel business model typically charges the highest per-night rate of all the kennel models. Up-charging for add-on services is typical, which adds revenue with little or no additional expenses.

The overwhelming majority of traditional kennels are located on the property where the owner lives. This is not just for convenience; this is to assure there is someone nearby at all times. The only safe alternative to this is for a facility to hire an overnight attendant or to include living quarters for an on-site employee.

HYBRID BOARDING
A third boarding kennel model is a hybrid between typical in-home boarding and a traditional kennel with runs. Hybrid kennels are freestanding facilities and guests are not staying in the owner's home. In this they are like traditional boarding kennels. But instead of the guests staying in segregated runs, as they would in a traditional

boarding kennel, the guests are free to enjoy the entire facility, or rooms, at will.

Hybrid boarding kennels are often outfitted to feel like a home, with the added benefit of more safety features than a residence provides. There may be sofas and chairs for the dogs, a TV in every room, and even rugs on the floor. But, unlike with in-home boarding, this facility will have entry and exit protocols overseen by staff and will most likely have more doors or gates acting as barriers against accidental escape.

Clients who want their dogs to interact with other dogs during their stay in a home-like facility, but with better security, might prefer this compromise between in-home and traditional.

For the business owner, hybrids may be the most challenging of all to run. The reservoir of dogs that can safely and reliably interact together unfettered is limited. Safety and security within the kennel is less at risk than in a home, but higher risk than in a traditional boarding kennel.

Dogs staying in this hybrid model should still have access to some segregated space for mealtimes and possibly sleeping. The facility needs to be large enough to accommodate these needs as well as provide that open, "homey" space. The initial investment is considerably higher than in-home boarding. You will likely need to hire staff to ensure the safety of each guest and provide them with the best professional care possible.

Overnight fees for a hybrid facility typically fall between those of in-home and traditional kennel facilities.

Regardless of which boarding model you choose, all new kennels need to build a loyal client base. And building a loyal client base starts with building trust.

Chapter 16.

Despite a plethora of rules, regulations, and ordinances, there is no legal entity tasked with certifying boarding kennels. There are a few private organizations trying to formalize certifications but they have no legal standing or government approval. The result is that customers are flying blind and taking a leap of faith when they initially bring their beloved pet to you. They are most likely relying on a recommendation or online reviews. They are simply hoping for the best. They are trusting that you will do best by their beloved pet.

Work every day to earn and retain that trust.

Sadly, there are less-than savory businesses calling themselves professional boarding kennels. They cut corners and do not provide the safest, cleanest, most ethical care. Don't be like them.

Be like the majority of kennel owners who want to do well by their clients and work hard to provide good service in a clean, safe environment. In the best-case scenarios, kennel facilities are as clean as, if not cleaner than, home; they are as safe as, if not safer than, home. Their staff is well-trained, well-educated professionals who are 100% dedicated to caring for the animals in their care. Be like them.

THE BUSINESS END OF RUNNING A BOARDING KENNEL
Because this is a business, the goal is to be profitable. Make sure your kennel can become profitable. That may sound self-evident but it is not. Here's why:

There is a kennel, which will go unnamed, that was built with no expenses spared. The owners bought a large multi-acre property and built a facility which, including the land, cost a rumored four million dollars. FOUR MILLION DOLLARS! They built out more than 100 runs and outfitted them to have all the bells and whistles: TV monitors so their guests wouldn't be bored, day beds and sofas for each dog, and an entrance and reception lobby that rivaled some five-star hotels for humans.

This kennel obviously needed to maintain a staff of dozens just to get through a normal day; busy holiday seasons required more. The cost to maintain just the staff was staggering. One would imagine that the debt on the facility was staggering, too. The financial obligation to maintain and manage this business was crushing.

To cover all their investment and expenses, their fees were based on the top-tier product they were offering.

The problem was that many people, at least in their particular area, were not interested in their dog having unfettered TV service and evening snacks; they certainly were not willing to pay a premium for it. Some of their potential clients also preferred their pets *not* get lost in the shuffle among 100+ other dogs.

After a very few years, the owners wanted (or needed) out. And they wanted to recoup their investment. In fact, they wanted to sell at a profit!

Now ask yourself, how many people do you suppose would pay even four million dollars for a business that was already underperforming? Who would be willing to take on a facility with that much overhead, that many challenges, and for that much debt?

Compare that to a much smaller boutique kennel that opened only a few miles away. Instead of 100+ runs they had 20. This kennel was designed to be small enough so that the owners could run it at capacity even if every employee was a no-show.

The owners kept the product simple and smart. And efficient. No TVs or sofas, but sturdy dog cots and a basic sound system for background music. The focus was on individual and personal care. Each dog got personal attention and play time with a human attendant every day. And, as this was part of their brand, the owners made sure customers knew this.

Of course, with a less luxurious facility, this kennel charged less than the four-million-dollar kennel down the road, but only by a few dollars less per dog, per night.

Staffing was minimal. They were well-paid and, more importantly, well-trained, so that during busy seasons the work was manageable and, while hectic, it was not overwhelming. In short, overhead was kept low.

The boarding kennel offered additional services such as grooming and had a small retail corner that could be overseen by whichever staff member was working reception that day. Classes were offered from time-to-time during slow seasons and were staffed by third-party vendors.

This boutique kennel was put on the market for sale late one summer. There were immediate offers. The six-figure asking price was met and was beyond the best ROI anything any kennel, of any size, had ever sold for in the entire state because when it sold, it sold with no real estate associated with it. The new business owners were obliged to pay rent to keep the kennel on site. This allowed the original owner to maintain an income from the kennel and additional ROI from the initial investment.

Who had the wiser business plan? Who considered profitability and sustainability?

IS IT SUSTAINABLE? CAN IT BE PROFITABLE?
The first step in ensuring your kennel will be sustainable is to make sure your location can support a kennel. Do your homework.

LOCATION

You need not live in immediate proximity to your target market, but you should have a good idea of the size of that market and know how far your potential customers will travel to reach you.

There are successful kennels in cities and there are successful kennels in the middle of nowhere. If your kennel is located in a city, your proximity and convenience to a large pool of potential customers is a plus; but you may have to charge a high nightly rate-per-dog to cover your expenses. Those prices may put your services out of reach for many in your potential client pool. You may face many competitors in your city. Consider how this will impact your business, but do not let this be the only factor in your decision-making process. If multiple grocery stores, pharmacies, or banks can co-exist in proximity to one another, and succeed, so can multiple boarding kennels. Just know what you are facing before you begin.

Alternatively, you could live and work out in the country with large play yards, room to spare, and no competition for miles. The further out you go, the lower your initial investment may be. You may be able to charge less and still be profitable. But your facility may feel too far off the beaten path for some people and the extra drive-time might put off some potential clients, making it harder, or take longer, to reach your goals.

Know your market, address the positives as well as the negatives of locating your kennel where you think you want to build; then adjust your plans and pricing accordingly.

Once you have established where to locate you kennel, start looking for the right property. Before you commit to any specific site or building, find out if you are permitted to have a kennel there. Do not assume. Get the facts and get them in writing. Even in rural or semi-rural areas, you could find that there are restrictions on the number of dogs allowed on your property or even having a boarding kennel at all.

EYES ON YOUR BOTTOM LINE AT ALL TIMES

To accurately price your services, you need to know your real numbers and you need to set realistic goals. Your income must outpace your expenses. Whether you are building a facility from scratch or investing in an existing one, know what that investment means in terms of its ROI.

For example, if your facility will have ten runs and cost $100,000 to build, each run, in essence, costs $10,000. How much do you need to charge to return the cost of that $10,000 + one-tenth of that beautiful lobby you envisioned + your salary (or that of your employees plus yours) + the cost of utilities, food, maintenance, taxes, and profit?

What about your mortgage or rent? The $100,000 you plan to spend on the kennel facility comes after, let's say, the $100,000 you will pay for the land it will sit on. Now each run needs to return a $200,000 investment!

You do not have to see a "return" on all that money at once. The mortgage is paid over time and your expenses are incurred over time. So your income needs to be viewed over time. Profitability does not need to be instantaneous, but you do need to cover your expenses and at some point your kennel should be profitable; otherwise, what's the point?

So let's say, for the sake of this argument, that the final amount you need to charge per night, every night, is $25. That is, if you charged $25 per night for 364 nights a year, you would cover your mortgage, any debt on your equipment, salaries (even yours), insurance, utilities, and taxes, and still be able to make a profit.

But let's be honest and realistic. Not each run will be filled each night; even the finest hotels in the world don't have 100% occupancy 100% of the time. So instead of $25, 365 nights a year, you may need to charge $35 or $45 for the 70% of the time each of those enclosures are in use. And 70% occupancy is beyond fantastic, especially in the early years.

You may immediately notice that the beautiful, large, airy lobby you were planning returns no income. That is not to say there is no worth to a beautiful, large, airy lobby; it's just that the lobby is a cost, not a revenue generator.

Find out, by doing good market research, if your target market will pay the rates you need to charge. If so, go for it. If not, adjust your expectations and plans. Don't forget to factor in add-ons and additional services that could generate income as well.

Do you see how the math works? These are the financials you need to calculate. Then you will be able to create and rely on calculated business plans.

YOUR FACILITY: PLANNING DOWN TO THE LAST ELECTRICAL OUTLET

Most people who want to own a boarding kennel have a vision of their ideal business including the size and scope of the facility they want. But as we all know, there's the fantasy and then there is the reality. Take time to plan the physical facility for your boarding kennel. Seek out advice from other kennel owners. Learn what works for them and what they wish they had done differently.

You may want to hire an architect to plan or at least draft the plans for your kennel. In fact, some jurisdictions will only permit plans for business facilities drafted by a licensed architect. Even if you are not mandated to hire an architect or drafter, you may want to do so anyway, especially if they have experience designing kennels, since you do not. In order to run efficiently, kennels have specific needs. There are a lot of details to consider that could get overlooked and may end up costing you more to alter or fix at a later date than the cost of hiring a professional.

Whether you design it yourself or hire an architect, just as was suggested for doggy daycare facilities in the previous chapter: KISS. Keep It Simple & Smart. And efficient. The more efficient your facility (and procedures and protocols), the fewer staff you will need.

Every boarding facility needs to consider:

- Size of each run (or crates for in-home boarding)
- Whether the runs have an outside enclosed component and if they do, what about Doggy doors?
- Flooring options
- Ceiling options
- Insulation for noise and temperature
- Secure and sanitary food prep area
- Bathing room
- Isolation room
- Rooms for future use (grooming/training/retail)
- Types of enclosures (if not runs)
- Water sources
- Placement of electrical points
- Storage space
- Size of hallways
- Outdoor areas
- Office space
- Security and security systems
- Bathrooms
- ADA compliance

- Lobby and reception (to suit logistics and protocols)
- Parking

SET UP YOUR BUSINESS

You can refer back to previous and the earliest chapters to see what are the basic business needs every business, including this one, needs. At a minimum you will need to

- Set up your legal business entity
- Establish a tax entity including workmen's comp account
- Arrange Bank accounts and payment portals
- Invest in scheduling software
- Enroll in a virtual payroll software platform

You should also:

- Build a relationship with regulators and stay in compliance
- Invest in a few cellphones and/or walkie talkies (so you can be in contact with your employees wherever they are in the facility)
- Set up security and CCTV systems
- Set up a rainy-day bank account for repairs and unexpected expenses. Make regular, even automation, deposits.

LIFE WHILE OWNING A BOARDING KENNEL

A day in the life of a kennel owner starts early, ends late, and is rarely repetitive or boring. Even if you choose to close to the public one day a week (no drop-offs, no pick-ups), the animals in your care still need to be tended to every day. You should expect to be late to many dinners. Kennel owners tend to pass up on holiday vacations and even family gatherings because holidays are kennels' busiest seasons.

In short, your life is no longer your own.

Burnout is a serious problem for kennel operators. So, a word to the wise: Eat when you can, drink lots of water, try to schedule your own "potty breaks," and set goals for getting sufficient hours of sleep nightly. Take personal time regularly.

If you have a partner, swap time off, even if it is only for a couple of hours a day. Try to schedule at least one day off a week. When you can afford to, hire staff.

Take care of yourself so you can take care of your guests, your clients, your staff, and your business.

WHAT DOES A TYPICAL DAY AT A TYPICAL BOARDING KENNEL LOOK LIKE?

Get ready, this may seem intense. Here's your daily checklist:

<u>Before the kennel opens to the public</u>
- ✓ Assign work to employees (over time they'll know what to do and just get to it)
- ✓ Dogs are let out for the first potty break of the day
- ✓ Runs are cleaned
- ✓ Water dishes are replaced with clean dishes and filled
- ✓ Dogs are fed
- ✓ After breakfast, food dishes are collected and washed
- ✓ Kitchen area is cleaned and restocked
- ✓ Dogs go out again
- ✓ Groomer and trainer arrive
- ✓ Discuss with your groomer their schedule for the day. Do the same with your trainer
- ✓ Head out to collect dogs (if you offer a pickup service)
- ✓ Prepare the dogs that are going home for pickup

Kennel opens to the public
- ✓ Dogs start going out, in turn, to the play yard for play time
- ✓ Check in dogs arriving for their stay
- ✓ Check in and out clients for grooming or additional services like training (this will continue all day)
- ✓ Check out dogs going home
- ✓ Runs are cleaned and sanitized after each guest leaves (even if they were already cleaned earlier that morning)
- ✓ Return calls, messages, and emails
- ✓ Take dogs out again, engage them in play or activities
- ✓ Check and refill water dishes
- ✓ Initiate calls (cold-calling, vendors, etc.)
- ✓ Work at daytime marketing and public relations (contacting the media, networking groups, community groups)
- ✓ Check and order supplies/accept deliveries
- ✓ Take dogs out again
- ✓ Clean public areas (office, reception, retail space, bathroom)
- ✓ Clean yards
- ✓ Clean entrance
- ✓ Clean runs continually after "accidents"

After the kennel closes to the public for the day
- ✓ Deal with the business end of your business (banking, reports, taxes, payroll, compliance)
- ✓ Refill water dishes
- ✓ Feed dogs
- ✓ Do laundry
- ✓ Collect dinner dishes and wash them
- ✓ Final clean of kitchen for the day
- ✓ Check all equipment
- ✓ Take out trash

- ✓ Hold classes or work on other secondary revenue streams
- ✓ Take dogs out for "last call"
- ✓ Evening marketing that does not involve contacting people at their workplace (social media, blog writing, etc.)

If that seems intense, that's because it is! An 8-hour day of doing business often translates into 18 hours of actual work.

And what happens when it's your slow season? You might think that this is the time to recharge your batteries, rest, or even take a vacation. Which you could, but only *after* you've:

- ✓ Taken care of the necessary repairs you didn't have time to do when your kennel was full

- ✓ Made the upgrades you've wanted to make but couldn't when there were so many guests on site

- ✓ Participated in any continuing education or trade conferences that you had no time for during the busy season

Then yes, you might be able to take some well-earned rest. Or even a vacation.

PROTOCOLS AND PROCEDURES
All kennels, regardless of size, format, or housing model, need serious, well-thought out, and consistently adhered-to procedures and protocols. The stakes and risks are high. It is your responsibility to mitigate those risks. The only way to do this is to think about every step of every task, determine what is the best way to complete each task, and make sure you do them to the highest standard possible, each time, all day, every day.

Pets in your care can suddenly present you with a host of issues and it is your responsibility to deal with each one.

You need a plan in case of sudden illness or accidents, whether or not you can reach that dog's owner. The same is true when dealing with natural disasters such as a hurricane. A power outage may be out of your control, but dealing with it *is* in your control. The same is true in case a client's return is delayed.

The best way to prevent bad situations from dissolving into disasters is to be prepared. And the best way to be prepared is to think of as many possible emergent scenarios you may face and determine how you will deal with them. Articulate those preventive measures and solutions and write a training manual or employee handbook.

Even if you are working by yourself, having a reference book may come in handy when faced with a serious problem that may throw you for a loop in the moment. The manual should also include the procedures and protocols you want followed for all aspects of working in your kennel, not just the emergency procedures.

Include all your rules and regulations. Articulate step-by-step instructions for every aspect having to do with caring for the dogs and include the step-by-steps for the more mundane tasks such as doing laundry. Include them all. Writing an employees' manual that contains all these things will save you time when time is of the essence and will make training new employees so much easier.

As the business owner, it is your responsibility to ensure that each member of your staff is qualified to care for your clients' pets. Be sure they are all on the same page with you and each other. This can only be achieved by training your staff well and insisting they learn, and adhere to, your clearly articulated and written protocols and procedures. Your employee manual should leave little room for misunderstanding by your employees.

Chapter 16.

Do not worry about having a perfect employee manual on day one. Over time, as you learn and gain experience, your manual will evolve. That is precisely how it should be.

There are virtually endless topics and subtopics your manual can and should include. At the very least it should address these:

HEALTH AND SAFETY PROTOCOLS TO ADDRESS
- Required immunizations and animal wellness standards
- Pest control for animals and in the kennel facility
- Arrival and departure protocols
- Food and feeding protocols
- Allowing, or not, toys or items brought from home
- Medications and their dispensing
- Illness or injury while at the kennel
- Emergency situations
- Emergency evacuations

ALSO SPELL OUT
- Daily schedule and feeding protocols
- Equipment supplied (beds, blankets)
- Cleaning schedules
- Cleaning protocols

BE SURE YOUR STAFF AND CLIENTS UNDERSTAND
- Your fee structure and hours of operation
- Fees and protocols for secondary services such as grooming or training, especially if a third party provides them

YOUR STAFF SHOULD BE CLEAR ABOUT
- Wages and pay schedule
- Continuing education expectations
- Standards of work
- Scope of work for each position

Detail how you want things done such as *how* you want enclosures cleaned (not just "clean runs"), *how* you want animals taken in and out of runs, *how* feeding should be done safely, etc. If you want your clean towels folded a certain way or food dishes washed a certain way you cannot expect your employees to know these things if you don't explain, demonstrate, and train them. Putting them in writing gives your employees a manual to refer to and a standard by which they can check themselves and you can evaluate them.

Reinforce to your staff that there are some rules and regulations that local authorities mandate and that these are absolutely non-negotiable.

The rules that you create are also to be followed explicitly because they are, in your professional opinion, the best way to ensure the health, safety, and well-being of your staff, your clients, and, most importantly, the pets in your care. However, as a good leader, be open to suggestions from staff about improving your processes and protocols. There is always room for improvement and any employee who has taken the time to think about this in their off time should be listened to.

Business set up? Check. Facility? Check. Protocols? Check. Your vision is coming together. Now what? Now, take the time to step back and see your business as others will see it. What do you need to do to create a client base?

BRANDING
Clients will not magically appear. People need to know about you in order to find you. You need to stand out from all the other pet service providers you are competing with. Build a brand. This will include your kennel's name, tagline, logo, and mission statement.

Chapter 16.

Remember, branding starts from knowing precisely who you are, what your business is, what needs does it fill, and what makes you different (better).

<u>NAMING YOUR BOARDING KENNEL BUSINESS</u>
It may seem as if all the great names for boarding kennels have been used already. That's a fair assessment. Finding a domain might be an even bigger problem, There can be many Puppy Palaces, but only one PuppyPalace.com.

As you become better known, the name on the marquee becomes less and less relevant. So while you want the "right" name, do not stress overly much about it. Choose something simple such as Main Street Kennels (if the domain is available and if your kennel is located on Main Street) or just use your name: Sally's Pet Boarding (unless there is already a boarding kennel named for their owner, Sally). You could modify a common kennel name with yours: Sally's Puppy Palace.

<u>TAGLINE AND MISSION STATEMENT</u>
Do not overlook the marketing value of a succinct mission statement and tagline. A short, well-crafted mission statement should tell the reader or listener precisely who you are and why they should want to be your client. Your tagline should fit on all your marketing materials. Be able to pitch your business in 30 seconds or less

<u>LOGO</u>
A clear, original logo that can be easily reproduced is a great marketing tool. Use it liberally. Wearing around town a t-shirt with a distinct logo and a memorable tagline can generate a lot of interest and business for a very small cost.

MARKETING
If you want to be a trusted member of the community, you need to be part of the community. Take part in community

events. Rent a booth at your local fairs, support your local civic clubs, network, and connect with fellow business owners regularly. Even though many of these events typically take place during the day, which is when you need to be caring for your guests, they are worth the effort.

MARKETING AVENUES TYPICAL TO THE INDUSTRY

<u>WEBSITE</u>
Make your kennel sound both professional and appealing. Don't forget to add as much information about your kennel as possible. Include your policies, prices, hours of operation, and short bios of you and your staff. You may be able to reduce the number of phone calls from prospective clients asking basic questions by clearly publicizing this information.

Have your boarding contract, liability release, and a photo release (for any photos you take while their pets are with you) on your website and require that clients sign them before accepting their reservations for their pet.

<u>SOCIAL MEDIA</u>
Either get in the habit of posting to social media regularly or hire someone to do it for you. Post good quality content only. Never publicly disclose any personal details about the pets or their owners. Cross-post to several social media platforms.

<u>LOCAL AND NOT SO LOCAL MEDIA OUTLETS</u>
Engage with your local and regional news outlets by pitching them suggested stories and offering your facility as a place for them to create their own content. Offer yourself up as a dog expert and be willing to appear on air or be interviewed by news stations, newspapers, or on podcasts.

If you are extremely ambitious you might consider starting your own blog or podcast.

Chapter 16.

EXPANDING REVENUES BEYOND BOARDING

As if running a boarding kennel wasn't already a full-time commitment, you might be thinking about how to extract even more income from your business.

Add-on services can bring in additional income by attaching a fee to each service. You could choose to charge for extra walks, bedtime treats, or dispensing medications. But some clients may balk at these. You could always list them as additional fees or à la carte services and then choose to waive those fees (nice marketing play).

Other impactful additional revenue streams at your existing boarding kennel might include:

SPECIALTY BOARDING

By offering specialty boarding services that other kennels may want to avoid, you can make your kennel stand out. Here are a couple of suggested specialty services:

1. Weight loss programs. Adding a weight-loss spa and program can be a very profitable add-on. Learn all you can about safely helping pets lose weight before attempting this and if possible, work with a local vet.

2. Post-surgery recuperation and rehab. Sometimes it is not possible for pet owners to care properly for their pets following medical procedures. If you have the knowledge and experience and if you have the necessary equipment and isolation space, you could offer this as a specialty service.

The following are more typical services that boarding kennels offer to increase and expand revenue streams.

GROOMING

Hire a groomer. Most groomers are open to splitting their fees in lieu of having to pay to rent your grooming room. Or learn basic grooming and add simple grooming services to your à la carte menu of add-ons.

TRAINING WHILE BOARDING

Hire a trainer to train dogs while they are boarding with you. You can either hire them as employees or find a trainer willing to work on commission and split the fees. If you have an existing employee who has training experience, give them a chance and allow them time during their workday to train. Pay them accordingly.

RELOCATION SERVICES

To avoid added stress, some families choose to relocate and get settled before having their pets shipped out to join them. Offer pre-travel crate training, driving their dog to the airport, or do the entire shipping process and charge accordingly.

RETAIL SHOP

Add a retail component to your boarding business. If you have the room, set up a retail corner with a carefully curated selection of products. Alternatively, create an e-commerce store with items you can personally recommend.

OFFER CLASSES

If you have a room large enough to hold a few chairs, you can offer classes. The larger the room, the larger the number of students you can host. These could be pet-CPR, basic pet care, basic pet grooming, or lectures on animal nutrition or behavior. Either teach the classes yourself or hire a third party to teach them.

HOST ACTIVITIES

Dog clubs are always looking for nice places to hold dog-sports competitions. If your facility has what they are looking for, find out what they will pay to rent yours and compare that to how much of a disturbance that would be for your guests. The publicity within the pet world alone might make this worthwhile!

SCALE UP

Once you have maxed out your boarding capacity you may want to further scale up your business. Here are your options.

<u>PHYSICALLY EXPAND YOUR FACILITY</u>

Expanding an existing building is not as expensive as starting from scratch but it is a big undertaking and can be expensive. You may need to go through the permitting process again. And you will be running your business in a construction zone for a while. In the end you will have more space for more dogs.

<u>BUY OR RENT A LARGER PLACE</u>

Relocating is never easy and relocating a business is risky. Your clients may not travel further just to follow you. Of course, if the relocation improves their convenience or if the change is so minimal as to have little impact, this might be your best option for expansion.

<u>ESTABLISH A SECOND SITE</u>

Ideally you would want this second site to be close enough for you to manage effectively (even if you do need to hire an on-site manager for at least one of your locations), yet far enough away to expand your reach and bring in new clients and new business.

In many ways starting a second facility is like going back to square one and building a new business. But this time you have a mountain of experience telling you what worked and what didn't. You may also be able to share some of the back of house support and share some expenses between the two sites.

There is no limit on the number of locations you could own.

<u>FRANCHISE</u>
Just as was detailed in the previous chapter about doggy daycare businesses, franchising your successful boarding kennel can be a great way to scale up. Franchising is a proven method for creating a chain of businesses, but setting up and overseeing a franchise framework can be challenging. Just ask any hotel chain.

It is imperative that you consult with as many experienced franchise owners and attorneys who specializing in franchises as possible. Learn the true pros and cons of taking on this challenge. Special attention needs to be paid to the specific needs and risks of caring for live animals when developing the framework for creating and selling businesses over which you will not have direct control.

Second only to protecting the animals, protecting your brand is critical, if you go the franchise route. Never forget what it took to become successful. Don't give it away too easily and never let future possibilities damage your brand today.

BITS AND PIECES FOR BUILDING BETTER BOARDING KENNELS
- Petcare is built on trust. Your reputation for trustworthiness is priceless. You can rarely recover from a bad reputation. Protect yours.

- A clean and odorless kennel will always win out over glitz and glamour. Put cleanliness before bells and whistles.

- Recognize that your neighbors may fear the traffic, noise, and smells a boarding facility may bring. Be a good neighbor by minimizing any imposition your business may bring to bear on them.

Chapter 16.

- Stay in compliance with all laws and guidelines.

- Know your target audience. Select and price your services accordingly.

- Always be friendly. If you are not friendly to your clients, they may not believe you will be kind and friendly to their pets.

- Always be professional. Your clients are counting on your knowledge and professionalism.

- Invest in your employees, even your temporary workers. They are doing a ridiculously hard job and the quality of their work reflects on you. Support them and they will support you.

- Don't forget to take care of yourself. Owning a boarding kennel can take over your life and burn you out. If you burn out, who will take care of your guests?

SUMMING UP

The recommendations in this book are not finite. Every good entrepreneur knows, or soon learns, that running a business is an on-going, evolving process and there is always more to learn.

Keep learning by enrolling in continuing education classes. Attend industry events and conferences. Connect with others in the field. Share what you know and they will, too.

The 5 most important take aways I hope you have gotten from this book are:

1. Do your research.
2. Plan well; have contingency plans.
3. Be professional.
4. Build trust.
5. You can do this.

ACKNOWLEDGMENTS AND THANKS

My career in the pet industry, and this book, would never have come to fruition without the support and mentorship from so many people.

Before all else, I thank my family. I hope I have been able to instill in my children not only a love of animals, but the courage to go after the careers and the lives they want, even when it's a little scary.

My entry into entrepreneurship would have been impossible without the guidance of my husband, Boaz, who advised me as I wrote my first business plans and taught me everything I now know, and now love, about creating and relying on budgets. Who knew that a girl who suffered through math in school would turn into a numbers nerd, or that underneath all that non-profit shell was a hard-core entrepreneur?

I am indebted to my beta readers who gave of their time and were gems for reading drafts that, in hindsight, were horrible. Thank you, Shannan Muscato, who took time from her own writing to help me with mine. Thanks to Nicole and Betsy, too.

And thank you Christine and Oren, the best editors any writer could ever hope for!

I want to thank all those who shared with me their knowledge of pet care and the pet industry starting with Denise and Arye Cass, whose Dog Farm was my introduction to boarding kennels and professional pet care. What great examples they and their kennel were!

So many other people (too numerous to include them all)

taught me along the way, both by good and bad example. My hope is that I have taken all those lessons and presented them here in a clear and encouraging way to help you, dear reader, do well for yourselves in business.

I wish you success.

Happy tails!

www.ingramcontent.com/pod-product-compliance
Lightning Source LLC
Chambersburg PA
CBHW051413090426
42737CB00014B/2649